THE EIFFEL TOWER

TIMELESS MONUMENT

BY BENJAMIN PEYREL

**Éditions
de La Martinière**

CONTENTS

ONE HUNDRED
AND THIRTY YEARS
OF INNOVATION

It is almost as though we've grown too accustomed to it. For the last one hundred and thirty years, the Eiffel Tower's 984 feet of iron latticework have majestically crowned Paris's skyline. Familiar, unchanging, obvious... So obvious that we sometimes forget about the intellectual, technical, and persuasive prowess that it took to build and keep the Tower in the heart of this city of stone. So familiar that we often overlook the heroic efforts that now enable us to touch the clouds.

One hundred and thirty years after its birth, the Eiffel Tower has become the indisputable symbol of France's capital city and its pride and joy. Over 300 million visitors from all over the world have climbed its uprights, anchoring the monument a little deeper each time in the world's collective imagination. But before becoming the unquestionable icon without which Paris wouldn't really be Paris anymore, the Tower was first and foremost a technical feat, the symbol of an artistic turning point, and the embodiment of a changing world. Both the witness of an era and eternally modern. In order to appreciate what makes the Eiffel Tower,

"AT ONCE USELESS AND IRREPLACEABLE"

as the philosopher Roland Barthes wrote, we must go back in time to the mid-1890s.

The 19th century has yet to breathe its last, but the 20th century is already looming on the horizon. At the end of the decade, France will host a Universal Exhibition. After losing the Franco-Prussian War and part of its territory along with it, this is France's opportunity to restore its rather tarnished image and to show the world its renewed greatness through the ingenuity of its scholars, industrialists, and inventors.

PAGE 2
The Eiffel Tower viewed
from the Champ-de-Mars,
at the time of the Universal
Exhibition in 1889.

PAGE 3
The Tower illuminated,
viewed from the
Palais de Chaillot on
the Trocadéro hill.

Such is the rather ambivalent role of universal exhibitions: to celebrate a shared faith in scientific and technological progress all the while flaunting one's power and national brilliance to one's neighbors. The new Republic, which is also celebrating the one hundredth anniversary of the French Revolution, needs something spectacular, something that will fill its citizens with pride and spark awe in its foreign visitors. That something will be a 984-foot-tall tower.

To be perfectly honest, the concept isn't exactly new. Ever since the beginning of the 19th century, the British, the Americans, and even the French have flirted with and sometimes sketched out ideas for such a structure made of stone or metal. But nobody has dared tackle this colossal challenge. Convinced by his inner circle and selected by the Exhibition's organizers, Gustave Eiffel will be the man to undertake this Herculean task and turn the dream into reality. A visionary and prolific engineer renowned for his work on bridges and viaducts, he will successfully raise his tower on

"IRON MUSE OF A NEW WORLD"

the banks of the Seine River in just over two years. It is a triumph for metal architecture, the booming discipline of calculations and scientific principles and of engineers and trailblazers. A structure of that height would never have been feasible with stone. Such a short construction time would never have been possible using the old techniques. Architects would never have dared such an ode to empty space, transparency, and futility. As the writer of the time Jules Simon comments,

"THIS MASTERPIECE IN BUILDING ART AT THE DAWN OF THE 20th CENTURY SYMBOLIZES THE SHIFT INTO THE IRON AGE."

As the icon of a world of progress in which technology reigns supreme, it is only natural that the Tower offends some nostalgic and slightly obstinate souls, for whom it is a source of dread or even rage. This "gigantic factory chimney" that "even the commercialized America wouldn't want on her shores" crushes "Notre-Dame, the Sainte-Chapelle, the Saint-Jacques Tower, the Louvre, the Dome of the Invalides, and the Arc de Triomphe with

OPPOSITE
At the foot of the Tower. Photograph by Pierre Jahan.

1887–1889

**2 YEARS, 2 MONTHS, AND 5 DAYS.
THE CONSTRUCTION TIME WAS A VERITABLE
TECHNICAL AND ARCHITECTURAL FEAT**

its barbarous mass," protest several great names in art and literature. For them the Eiffel Tower will disfigure the French capital. One hundred and thirty years later, it has become the universal emblem of that same city. Not everyone is born to be a visionary...Eiffel, on the other hand, was just that.

EVERY YEAR, OVER 6 MILLION EAGER VISITORS PAY A KIND OF CONTINUING AND SUBCONSCIOUS HOMAGE TO HIS MANY TALENTS.

Known first and foremost as an engineer, he managed to design and build this giant Erector set using the most innovative technologies of the time in under nine hundred days. However, he was also an astute businessman who successfully transformed this "beautifully useless" and controversial object of curiosity into a must-see site that continues to enjoy renewed success with the general public to the extent that it is one of the rare monuments to operate without public funding. Not only that, but Eiffel was also a scientist who transformed his Tower into a veritable laboratory and the birthplace of new techniques and technologies. Finally, he was a visionary who fought to save his Tower, which was initially doomed for destruction, thereby enabling "this industrial masterpiece to escape from the century that had created it," in the words of art historian Henri Loyrette.

Of course, the Tower's longevity is not solely thanks to Eiffel. Over the past one hundred and thirty years, thousands of people have kept careful watch over the Iron Lady's future and wellbeing while continuously modernizing her to give visitors an unrivaled and unforgettable experience. Some of Eiffel's genius still infuses the brushes of the painter-acrobats who dance through Paris's sky every seven years to cover her with a new protective coat of paint. Some of Eiffel's genius continues to inform the precise movements of the dozens of technicians who meticulously check her elevators and devices every day – the Tower's arteries and lungs, in a manner of speaking. Some of Eiffel's genius inspires the employees of the SETE (*Société d'exploitation de la tour Eiffel*), the local public company tasked with managing the monument, who work daily to maintain and enhance it, along with the visitor's experience, all the while strengthening its status in France and abroad.

THE 300-METER
CHALLENGE

THE BUILDING OF THE EIFFEL TOWER

The date is January 8, 1887 and a dizzying countdown has begun in the heart of France's capital city. Edouard Lockroy (the Minister of Industry), Eugène Poubelle (the Prefect of the Seine's administrative department), and Gustave Eiffel have just signed the agreement entrusting Eiffel with the construction of a 984-foot-tall tower for the opening of the next Universal Exhibition.

This event has been set for May 5, 1889, and time is of the essence if the engineer is to pull off this extraordinary feat. Two years, two months, and five days later – just over a month before the deadline – the wager has been won.

Meanwhile, over the course of the intervening three winters and two summers, all of Paris bears witness to an astonishing game of Erector set that displays the virtuosity of Eiffel's engineers and their teams of workers. Crowds of onlookers flock to the foot of the Champ-de-Mars work site every day to observe the progress. The Tower seems to sprout up like some kind of metal tree from the loose soil on the banks of the Seine River before their very eyes. Of course, reality is much less poetic and organic. Everything related to the Tower's construction is based on science, careful calculations, and cutting-edge building techniques. The curvature of the uprights, for example, is mathematically determined to decrease wind resistance as much as possible. Likewise, the metal pieces must be assembled to within a fraction of an inch. Nearly all columnists of the time agree: it's a marvelous exploit in precision.

This achievement is made possible thanks to fifty engineers and

OPPOSITE
Gustave Eiffel (center) posing on the Tower construction site with fellow team members Salles, Nouguier and Sauvestre.

ABOVE

The Tower features
on every poster
and advertisement
– plainly the star of the
Universal Exhibition.

7 300

**METRIC TONS. THE WEIGHT
OF THE METAL FRAMEWORK**

draftsmen as well as several hundred workers, only some of whom are based on the actual work site. The Tower's assembly may appear fluid from afar, but the illusion resides in Eiffel's incredible organizational skills, which he has honed over the course of his career with projects such as the Garabit viaduct in Auvergne or the Maria Pia bridge over the Douro River in Portugal. Above all, however, the Tower's progress is the result of in-depth preparation work. All of the monument's 18,000 pieces are designed and created in Eiffel's workshop located at Levallois-Perret and arrive ready to be assembled. Once on site, the pieces are simply positioned and riveted together.

It's easier said than done. The 130 workers – or "chimney sweeps" as they are nicknamed – daily brave the cold, wind, and sometimes vertigo under the watchful eyes of veterans of great metal viaduct projects. In rather acrobatic working conditions, they hoist, pull, push, heat and strike to assemble the pieces. In ten months, the 187 feet up to the first floor are in place. It takes approximately the same amount of time to erect the elegant metal structure up to the intermediate platform's 640 feet located between the second and third floors. In barely one hundred more days, they reach the third floor. It then takes a good twenty days to put the finishing touches on the top of the Tower, including a control room, an office for Gustave Eiffel, the campanile, and the flag pole. On March 31, 1889 at approximately 2:30 pm, the French flag flies from the top of the Tower as twenty cannon shots resound through the Parisian sky.

I have just had the immense satisfaction of flying our country's flag from the tallest building that man has ever built, says Gustave Eiffel to his workers assembled at the foot of the Tower for the grand occasion. We have achieved our goal, but doing so was no small task on all of our parts, both intellectual and manual! It took great perseverance for my colleagues and me to prepare and coordinate the work, and it took just as much perseverance for you to execute our instructions despite the inclement weather, cold, and wind that you so often braved on this tall Tower! But once we started down this path, retreat was not an option. We had committed to doing something that many people had attempted or dreamed of, but nobody had yet accomplished. We had no choice but to keep our word, at the risk of compromising our nation's honor. And we kept it.

Gustave Eiffel, 31 March 1889

OPPOSITE
Work finished: on 31 March 1889, the French flag flies over the completed Tower.

FOLLOWING PAGE
Contract for the construction of the Eiffel Tower, signed by Messrs Eiffel, Poubelle and Lockroy on 8 January 1887.

Convention
relative à la Tour Eiffel.

———

Entre Monsieur Edouard **Lockroy**, Ministre du Commerce et de l'Industrie, Commissaire Général de l'Exposition Universelle de 1889, agissant au nom de l'État;

Monsieur Eugène **Poubelle**, Préfet de la Seine, agissant au nom de la Ville de Paris, ainsi qu'il y est autorisé par les délibérations du Conseil Municipal des 22 Octobre et 28 Décembre 1886 et cela dans les limites fixées par ces délibérations, qui resteront annexées aux présentes;

D'une part;

Et Monsieur **Eiffel**, Ingénieur-Constructeur, demeurant à Levallois-Perret, rue Fouquet, N° 42; agissant en son nom personnel;

D'autre part.

Ont été faites les conventions suivantes:

Article premier.

M᷑ Eiffel s'engage envers M le Ministre du Commerce & de l'Industrie, Commissaire Général

1887

JANUARY 8

THE AGREEMENT IS SIGNED
BETWEEN THE STATE, THE CITY
OF PARIS, AND GUSTAVE EIFFEL

JULY 1

COMPLETION OF THE FOUNDATIONS
AND BEGINNING OF THE METAL
STRUCTURE

1888

APRIL 1

COMPLETION OF THE FIRST FLOOR
AND BEGINNING OF THE ASCENT
TO THE SECOND FLOOR

AUGUST 14

COMPLETION OF THE SECOND
FLOOR AND BEGINNING
OF THE THIRD

1889

FEBRUARY 24

COMPLETION OF THE THIRD FLOOR

MARCH 31

CLOSING OF THE WORK SITE AND
INAUGURATION OF THE EIFFEL
TOWER

MAY 5

OPENING OF THE UNIVERSAL
EXHIBITION

MAY 15

OPENING OF THE TOWER
TO THE GENERAL PUBLIC

Temporary buildings for the Universal Exhibition
at the foot of the Eiffel Tower.

In the name of France's unsung good taste and her art and history which are under threat, we – writers, painters, sculptors, architects, passionate admirers of Paris's beauty which is as yet unmarred – protest with all our might and outrage the erection of the useless and monstrous Eiffel Tower in the very heart of our capital city. Indeed, in a display of common sense and justice as is so often the case, popular malignity has already christened it "The Tower of Babel.

Artists against the Eiffel Tower, excerpt from the letter to Monsieur Alphand, published on February 14, 1887 in *Le Temps*

The colossal has a certain attraction and charm to which theories of the ordinary arts are scarcely applicable. Take, for instance, the pyramids of Egypt. Was it their artistic value that inspired man's imagination? What are they, after all, if not man-made hills? And yet, what visitor remains indifferent in their presence? What visitor is not filled with irresistible admiration? And what is the source of that admiration if not the immense scale of the construction and its grandeur? The Tower will be the tallest structure ever built by man. Will it not then be grandiose in its own way? Why would that which is admirable in Egypt be considered hideous and ridiculous in Paris? Try as I might, I must admit that it escapes my understanding.

Gustave Eiffel's response

OPPOSITE
Ingenious caissons fed with compressed air serve to keep out the water while constructing the Tower's foundations on the Seine side.

ASSEMBLY

FROM INITIAL DIGGING TO COMPLETING THE FOUNDATIONS

JANUARY 28 – JULY 1, 1887

In a report published after the end of the Universal Exhibition, its commissioner general, the engineer Alfred Picard, recalls some of the questions leading up to the decision regarding the siting of the Eiffel Tower. "Was it really wise to build it in the Seine valley? Shouldn't it be placed higher up on a hill that would naturally elevate it like a kind of pedestal?"

For a while, the plan is to build the monument on the other side of the Seine at the top of Chaillot hill, but the Trocadero area's deeply excavated earth soon undercuts that idea. Instead, the Tower will be built on the Champ-de-Mars at the very entrance to the Universal Exhibition. That being said, the choice isn't without its share of technical difficulties.

The side facing the *Ecole Militaire* doesn't present any problems: after digging a few yards into the ground, workers reach a bed of gravel and then pour a six-and-a-half-foot-thick layer of concrete upon which two of the Tower's stone pillar bases will rest. The side facing the Seine, however, proves more complex as the monument's base extends below the riverbed.

To prevent seepage, Eiffel employs a method that he has previously used for bridge construction: watertight metal caissons injected with compressed air that enable workers to operate below the water level. The technique is so effective that in a mere five months, the four pillar bases are built and joined together by walls. Together, they form a square measuring 410 feet per side. On July 1, 1887, assembly of the metal structure can commence.

It took Eiffel's construction teams five months to complete the foundations
and columns for the 984ft (300m) tall Tower.

18 038

THE NUMBER OF IRON COMPONENTS

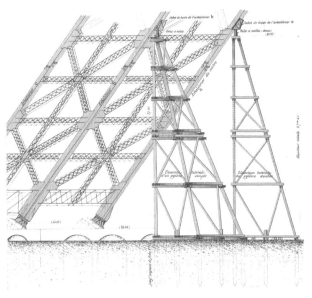

Rugged scaffolding
supports the construction
of the Tower's four
columns as the structure
rises by stages above
the Champ-de-Mars.

FROM THE FOUNDATIONS TO THE FIRST FLOOR
JULY 1, 1887 – APRIL 1, 1888

Erecting the structure is undoubtedly the most complex part of the entire project, and for good reason, as Eiffel and his engineers must confront a crucial problem: the gradient of the sixteen trusses. These large iron tubes assembled in square sections are the most important parts of the Tower's primary structure. These trusses support the entire structure and must meet at the first floor in order to ensure its stability. Even the tiniest difference in gradient at the base could prove disastrous higher up. In order to avoid such a catastrophe, hydraulic jacks are installed on the pedestals and the workers use

"sand boxes" on the wooden scaffolding. The two techniques enable them to adjust the position of the frame to within a fraction of an inch.

On December 7, 1887, the four pillars are joined together by the installation of the four large 77-ton-girders on the first floor – to within a fraction of an inch! The jacks and "sand boxes" are then replaced by steel wedges that definitively ensure the monument's leveling. The Tower now has a solid base. A little over four months later, on April 1, 1888, the first floor's platform is complete. The project is right on track.

FROM THE FIRST
TO THE SECOND FLOOR

APRIL 1 – AUGUST 14, 1888

In order to hoist themselves up to the first floor (187 feet above the Champ-de-Mars), the workers install twelve temporary wooden scaffolds to reinforce and erect the pillars. After that, four large scaffolds are used to brace the four large first-floor girders while they are attached to the structure. The parts are hauled up by mobile steam cranes moving along the rails of the future elevators.

To reach the second floor, however, a different method is used. Instead of intermediate scaffolds, small wooden platforms are installed around the four pillars and are progressively moved upward as the Tower climbs toward the sky. A steam-powered freight elevator is installed on the first floor. The workers are making good progress. In under six months, they reach the second floor's altitude of 377 feet above the ground.

The work site, which has become a strolling destination and a veritable attraction for all of Paris, gradually disappears from sight. To satisfy people's curiosity, the Grévin Museum is called upon to install sets with life-size mannequins of the workers to give onlookers an idea of the ballet playing out in the sky above. A love affair between the capital's inhabitants and the Tower has begun.

OPPOSITE
As construction advances, cranes mounted on the supporting columns hoist 18,038 iron components to the points where they will be assembled.

ABOVE
The Eiffel Tower is truly a work of *dentelle de fer* (iron lacework).

A critical moment in construction: installing the beams that will link the Tower's four supporting columns to form the first floor. The accuracy of all parts is measured in fractions of an inch.

As construction moves forward, the Tower sheds its wooden scaffolding.

FROM THE SECOND
TO THE THIRD FLOOR

AUGUST 14, 1888 – FEBRUARY 24, 1889

High above the Champ-de-Mars, the assembly process is beginning to look like an exploit in acrobatics, with the workers forced to battle inclement weather, vertigo, and the wind in less-than-ideal working conditions.

After the second floor, the Tower begins to resemble a pylon and the number of cranes (which must now use an exterior frame) is reduced to two. In a fog of tar and coal illuminated by showers of sparks, the work continues at a pace of approximately sixty-six feet per month.

On November 30, the assembly of the intermediate platform between the second and third floors is complete, followed by the third floor itself on February 24, 1889. The Iron Lady now measures 906 feet in height. All that remains is to crown her with a few finishing touches and a flag pole from which the French flag will proudly fly, 1,024 feet above Paris's soil.

It is March 31, 1889 and one of mankind's most formidable adventures has just come to a close. The Eiffel Tower is born; now the legend can begin.

OPPOSITE PAGE
By 31 October 1888, construction has passed beyond the second floor level and the Tower now punctuates the Paris skyline.

FOLLOWING TWO PAGES
A celebration of the age of steel, the dominant material in the period of the 1889 Universal Exhibition, as displayed here in the *Galerie des Industries Diverse*.

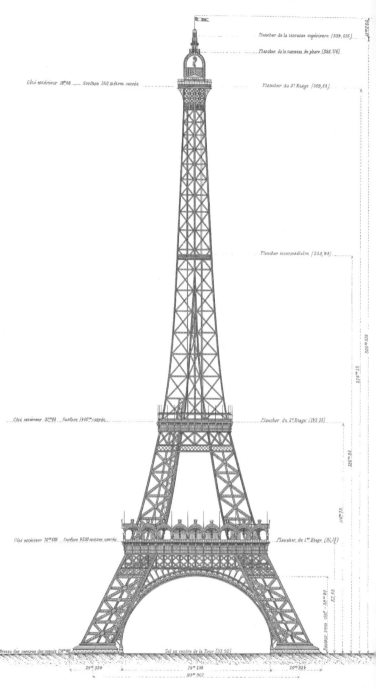

312

**METERS (1,024 FEET). THE INITIAL
HEIGHT OF THE EIFFEL TOWER**

LE MONDE ILLUSTRÉ

JOURNAL HEBDOMADAIRE

ABONNEMENT POUR PARIS ET LES DÉPARTEMENTS
Un an, 24 fr.; — Six mois, 13 fr.; — Trois mois, 7 fr.; — Un numéro, 50 c.
Le volume semestriel, 12 fr. broché. — 17 fr. relié et doré sur tranche.
LA COLLECTION DES 32 ANNÉES FORME 64 VOLUMES

32ᵉ Année. — N° 1650. — 10 Nov. 1888

Directeur : **M. ÉDOUARD HUBERT**

DIRECTION ET ADMINISTRATION, 13, QUAI VOLTAIRE
Toute demande d'abonnement non accompagnée d'un bon sur Paris
ou sur la poste, toute demande de numéro à laquelle ne sera pas joint le
montant en timbres-poste, seront considérées comme non avenues. —
On ne répond pas des manuscrits envoyés.

L'EXPOSITION UNIVERSELLE. — ÉTAT ACTUEL DE LA TOUR EIFFEL (178 MÈTRES) ET DES CONSTRUCTIONS ENVIRONNANTES.

Photographie de M. GIARD (31 octobre 1888.)

GREAT INVENTIONS OF THE TIME

1876
INVENTION OF THE
FOUR-STROKE ENGINE
AND THE TELEPHONE

1879
INVENTION OF THE
INCANDESCENT LAMP

1885
DISCOVERY OF THE
VACCINE FOR RABIES

1886
PARIS INTRODUCES ITS
FIRST ELECTRIC STREET
LIGHTS

1887
THE CONSTRUCTION
OF THE EIFFEL TOWER
BEGINS

1888

DISCOVERY OF
ELECTROMAGNETIC
WAVES

1889

THE EIFFEL TOWER'S
CONSTRUCTION IS
COMPLETE

1890

CLÉMENT ADER
TAKES OFF IN THE FIRST
AIRCRAFT, *ÉOLE*

1895

INVENTION OF THE FILM
PROJECTOR

1897

INVENTION OF
WIRELESS TELEGRAPHY

AN ENGINEERING DREAM MADE REAL

It may bear the name of only one man, but there were in fact a great many who cradled the Iron Lady in her infancy. Truth be told, the idea of a tall tower had been brewing for a while.

As early as 1833, the English engineer Richard Trevithick flirts with the idea of building a column measuring 1,000 feet in height on English soil. Thirty years later, the Americans Clarke and Reeves even submit a relatively well-thought-out idea to the organizers of the Universal Exhibition in Philadelphia in 1876. The proposal is shut down. The idea nonetheless continues to gain ground. An associate of the architect Jules Bourdais, the French engineer Amédée Sébillot, has been working since 1881 on the idea of a "Sun Tower" made of granite with a light source at the top that could illuminate Paris.

In short, in the mid-1880s, dreams of grandeur are not unique to Gustave Eiffel. In fact, he is so focused on his bridges and viaducts that the thought doesn't even occur to him. Two of his company's managers, Maurice Koechlin and Émile Nouguier, suggest the idea in 1884. He initially refuses their proposal before agreeing to it once the design has been revised. He will eventually appropriate it by buying the patent from his employees. So, who were the men behind the Eiffel Tower?

At first much criticized, the Tower grew to be an unbeatable attraction,
and people rushed to visit the site.

GUSTAVE EIFFEL

Although Gustave Eiffel doesn't initiate the project strictly speaking, the Tower would probably never have existed without him. Once he is convinced of the project's merit, the man referred to as the "iron magician" will literally bring it to life and see it through: convincing politicians of its value, countering its critics one by one, orchestrating one of the most ambitious work sites ever conceived, and fighting to ensure the longevity of the monument, his business, and his name… As Eiffel nears his sixtieth birthday, this project will mark the grand finale of the dazzling and exceptional career of this brilliant engineer, peerless organizer, and genius businessman.

MAURICE KOECHLIN

Koechlin is the man behind the initial drawing, without whom Paris's skyline would perhaps seem rather empty to us today. On June 6, 1884, the head of Eiffel's design office jots down a few calculations and roughly sketches out a very tall tower that could "add a certain appeal" to the Universal Exhibition. To indicate the scale of the monument he has in mind, he even draws the carefully stacked silhouettes of Notre-Dame, the Statue of Liberty, the Arc de Triomphe, three Place Vendôme obelisks, and a six-story building on one side. As for the Tower itself, it still resembles a tall openwork pylon. The pillars, which are spread out at the base and join up at the top, are connected to one another by five girders placed every 164 feet. It may look a bit stiff, but the basic idea is there and after Stephen Sauvestre's revisions, it will eventually win Eiffel over. After ceding his rights to Eiffel, the Alsatian engineer will supervise the construction of the Tower and will receive the Legion of Honor at its inauguration. Four years later, he will follow in Gustave Eiffel's footsteps as head of the company.

OPPOSITE
The original drawing for the 984ft (300m) tall tower, as visualized by Maurice Koechlin.

STEPHEN SAUVESTRE

The artist in the group, Sauvestre manages to turn the clever but rather awkward idea put forward by Nouguier and Koechlin into a proposition that will eventually seduce Eiffel and the general public. When the illustrious engineer sends his two employees back to the drawing board, they turn to the company's official architect for help. As he works, the Tower becomes more elegant and is transformed from a simple pylon into an architectural project and a work of art.
He first adds the four stonework pedestals followed by decorative monumental arches to the four pillars and the first floor. He then streamlines the structure and reduces it to three floors, which he enlivens with archways and glass-walled viewing spaces for visitors. Lastly, he completes the slender silhouette with a beautiful dome. The Iron Lady is ready to make her grand début.

ÉMILE NOUGUIER

"This difficult task required a man like him and I can say in all fairness that it is especially thanks to him that this 300-meter-tall Tower exists at all." In 1890, this is how Émile Nouguier describes Gustave Eiffel to the "Society for the Encouragement of National Industry" [*Société d'encouragement pour l'industrie nationale*]. The task may have required a man like Eiffel, but it also needed someone like Nouguier. After joining the company in 1876, this graduate of the *Ecole des Mines* soon becomes the head of the production planning department. He is the one to share the tower idea with his friend Koechlin, with whom he makes the first calculations and considers the initial set of questions. "It was an interesting problem because it was not only a matter of resolving engineering challenges," he later said, "but we also had to meet them without exceeding a certain budget, which had to be respected at all costs." In the end, the Tower (whose assembly Nouguier would design and oversee) only cost 1.5 million francs more than the initial quote of 6.5 million.

OPPOSITE
An extraordinary interweaving of metallic trelliswork.

BEHIND THE SCENES

To the Parisians walking by the work site every day, it is as though the Tower is sprouting up before their very eyes of its own volition, and for good reason. There aren't thousands of busy workers racing about the base of the Tower, no enormous plumes of smoke coming from forges or production areas. In order to save time and avoid mistakes, Eiffel has chosen to limit work on the Champ-de-Mars as much as possible. Instead, the bulk of the work takes place in his Levallois workshop, where his company has been based since 1867. At the workshop, approximately forty draftsmen will spend eighteen months creating more than 5,300 preliminary drawings.

"We created drawings of each individual component using calculations and logarithms to determine the position of the rivet holes that would connect one component to another," Gustave Eiffel would later explain in his work entitled *The 300-Meter Tower* published in 1900. "The position of each hole was calculated to a tenth of a millimeter."

This painstaking task is followed by another to be carried out by the "floor boys." At a rate of 330 to 440 tons per month, this team of 150 to 200 workers cuts, drills, and assembles the pieces of iron from the Fould-Dupont foundry and factory in Meurthe-et-Moselle into sections measuring sixteen feet in length. More than two thirds of the Tower's 2.5 million rivets are installed in this Parisian suburb with the greatest fastidiousness in order to limit errors or modifications as much as possible. Thanks to this scientific and highly organized system, the Tower quickly reaches the clouds. This stroke of genius will also bestow Eiffel with the incredibly rare privilege of seeing a street named after him during his lifetime.

2 500 000

THE NUMBER OF RIVETS (SMALL FIXINGS THAT CONNECT THE METAL COMPONENTS)

ABOVE
Producing the puddle iron at the steelworks.

FOLLOWING TWO PAGES
One of many illustrative spreads from Gustave Eiffel's book
La Tour de 300 Metres (The 300-Meter Tower), published in 1900.

ENSEMBLES ET DÉTAILS DES ARCS DÉCO[

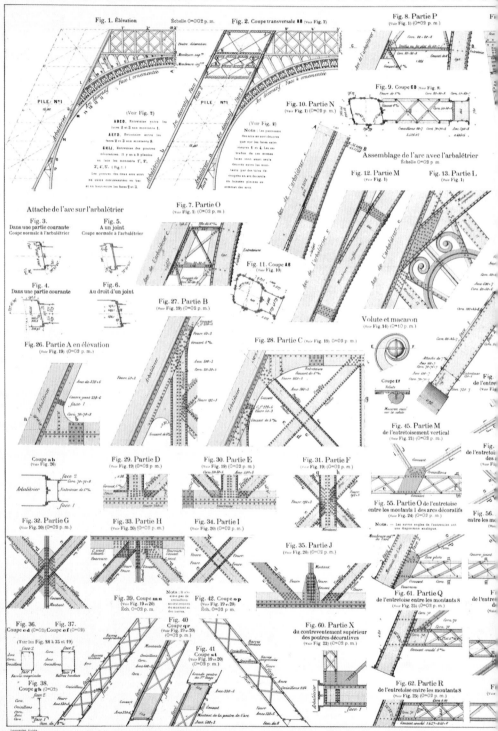

Fig. 1. Élévation — Échelle 0=002 p. m.

Fig. 2. Coupe transversale AB (Voir Fig. 1)

Fig. 8. Partie P (Voir Fig. 1) (0=05 p. m.)

Fig. 9. Coupe CD (Voir Fig. 8)

Fig. 10. Partie N (Voir Fig. 1) (0=02 p. m.)

Assemblage de l'arc avec l'arbalétrier — Échelle 0=02 p. m.

Fig. 12. Partie M (Voir Fig. 1)

Fig. 13. Partie L (Voir Fig. 1)

Attache de l'arc sur l'arbalétrier

Fig. 3. Dans une partie courante — Coupe normale à l'arbalétrier

Fig. 5. A un joint — Coupe normale à l'arbalétrier

Fig. 7. Partie O (Voir Fig. 1) (0=02 p. m.)

Fig. 11. Coupe AB (Voir Fig. 10)

Fig. 4. Dans une partie courante

Fig. 6. Au droit d'un joint

Fig. 27. Partie B (Voir Fig. 19) (0=02 p. m.)

Volute et macaron (Voir Fig. 14) (0=10 p. m.)

Fig. 26. Partie A en élévation (Voir Fig. 19) (0=02 p. m.)

Fig. 28. Partie C (Voir Fig. 19) (0=02 p. m.)

Coupe ef — Volute

Fig. de l'entre

Fig. 45. Partie M de l'entretoisement vertical (Voir Fig. 21) (0=02 p. m.)

Fig. de l'entretoi des

Coupe ab (Voir Fig. 26)

Fig. 29. Partie D (Voir Fig. 19) (0=02 p. m.)

Fig. 30. Partie E (Voir Fig. 19) (0=02 p. m.)

Fig. 31. Partie F (Voir Fig. 19) (0=02 p. m.)

Fig. 55. Partie O de l'entretoise entre les montants 1 des arcs décoratifs (Voir Fig. 24) (0=02 p. m.)

Nota. — Les autres angles de l'entretoise ont une disposition analogue.

Fig. 56. entre les m (Vo

Fig. 32. Partie G (Voir Fig. 20) (0=02 p. m.)

Fig. 33. Partie H (Voir Fig. 20) (0=02 p. m.)

Fig. 34. Partie I (Voir Fig. 20) (0=02 p. m.)

Fig. 35. Partie J (Voir Fig. 20) (0=02 p. m.)

Fig. 61. Partie Q de l'entretoise entre les montants 8 (Voir Fig. 25) (0=02 p. m.)

Fig. de l'entre d

Fig. 36. Coupe cd (0=02)

Fig. 37. Coupe ef (0=02)

Fig. 39. Coupe mn (Voir Fig. 19 et 20) Éch. 0=02 p. m.

Fig. 42. Coupe op (Voir Fig. 19 et 20) Éch. 0=02 p. m.

Fig. 60. Partie X du contreventement supérieur des poutres décoratives (Voir Fig. 23) (0=02 p. m.)

Fig. 62. Partie R de l'entretoise entre les montants 8 (Voir Fig. 25) (0=02 p. m.)

(Voir les Fig. 28 à 35 et 19)

Fig. 40. Coupe qr (Voir Fig. 19 et 20) (0=02 p. m.)

Fig. 41. Coupe st (Voir Fig. 19 et 20) (0=02 p. m.)

Fig. 38. Coupe gh (0=02)

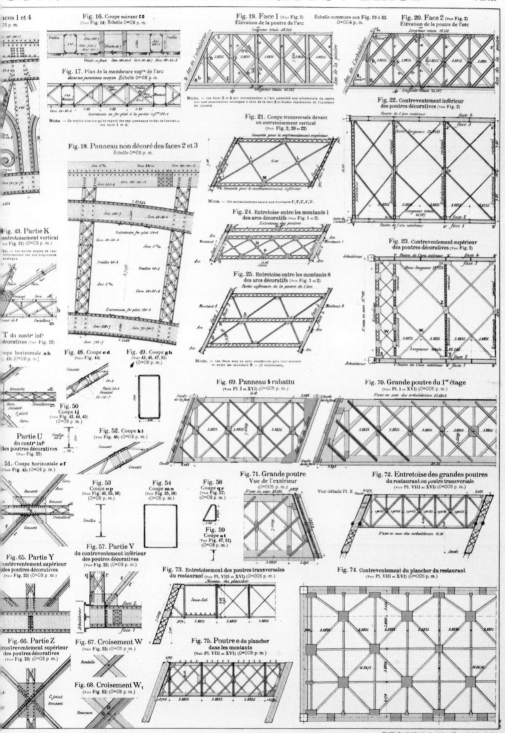

Fig. 16. Coupe suivant CD (Voir Fig. 14) Échelle 0ᵐ02 p. m.

Fig. 17. Plan de la membrure supᵉ de l'arc dans un panneau moyen Échelle 0ᵐ02 p. m.

Fig. 18. Panneau non décoré des faces 2 et 3 Échelle 0ᵐ03 p. m.

Fig. 19. Face 1 (Voir Fig. 1) Élévation de la poutre de l'arc

Fig. 20. Face 2 (Voir Fig. 2) Élévation de la poutre de l'arc

Échelle commune aux Fig. 19 à 25 0ᵐ004 p. m.

Fig. 21. Coupe transversale devant un entretoisement vertical (Voir Fig. 2, 20 et 22)

Fig. 22. Contreventement inférieur des poutres décoratives (Voir Fig. 2)

Fig. 23. Contreventement supérieur des poutres décoratives (Voir Fig. 2)

Fig. 24. Entretoise entre les montants 1 des arcs décoratifs (Voir Fig. 1 et 2)

Fig. 25. Entretoise entre les montants 8 des arcs décoratifs (Voir Fig. 1 et 2)

Fig. 43. Partie K Contretoisement vertical (Voir Fig. 21)

Fig. 48. Coupe c d (Voir Fig. 44)

Fig. 49. Coupe g h (Voir Fig. 43, 45, 47, 51) (0ᵐ05 p. m.)

Fig. 50. Coupe i i (Voir Fig. 43, 44, 45) (0ᵐ05 p. m.)

Fig. 52. Coupe k l (Voir Fig. 46) (0ᵐ02 p. m.)

Partie U du contrᵉ infᵉ des poutres décoratives (Voir Fig. 22)

Fig. 51. Coupe horizontale e f (Voir Fig. 45) (0ᵐ02 p. m.)

Fig. 53. Coupe o p (Voir Fig. 46, 55, 56) (0ᵐ05 p. m.)

Fig. 54. Coupe m n (Voir Fig. 55, 56) (0ᵐ05 p. m.)

Fig. 58. Coupe q r (Voir Fig. 57) (0ᵐ02 p. m.)

Fig. 59. Coupe s t (Voir Fig. 47, 51) (0ᵐ02 p. m.)

Fig. 57. Partie V du contreventement inférieur des poutres décoratives (Voir Fig. 22) (0ᵐ02 p. m.)

Fig. 65. Partie Y Contreventement supérieur des poutres décoratives (Voir Fig. 23) (0ᵐ02 p. m.)

Fig. 66. Partie Z Contreventement supérieur des poutres décoratives (Voir Fig. 23) (0ᵐ02 p. m.)

Fig. 67. Croisement W (Voir Fig. 23) (0ᵐ05 p. m.)

Fig. 68. Croisement W₁ (Voir Fig. 23) (0ᵐ05 p. m.)

Fig. 69. Panneau 5 rabattu (Voir Pl. I et XVI) (0ᵐ005 p. m.)

Fig. 70. Grande poutre du 1ᵉʳ étage (Voir Pl. I et XVI) (0ᵐ005 p. m.)

Fig. 71. Grande poutre Vue de l'extérieur (0ᵐ005 p. m.) Voir détails Pl. X

Fig. 72. Entretoise des grandes poutres du restaurant ou poutre transversale (Voir Pl. VIII et XVI) (0ᵐ005 p. m.)

Fig. 73. Entretoisement des poutres transversales du restaurant (Voir Pl. VIII et XVI) (0ᵐ005 p. m.)

Fig. 74. Contreventement du plancher du restaurant (Voir Pl. VIII et XVI) (0ᵐ005 p. m.)

Fig. 75. Poutre e du plancher dans les montants (Voir Pl. VIII et XVI) (0ᵐ005 p. m.)

ON THE WORK SITE
THE WORKERS' DAY-TO-DAY LIFE

If the construction of the Eiffel Tower advances at such a good clip, it is in large part thanks to the work done at the Levallois workshop before the components even reach the work site. On the Champ-de-Mars, however, that is no reason to be idle. Every day, approximately 130 workers receive components weighing up to three tons that arrive in large horse-drawn trucks. They are then transferred to carts and transported to the cranes that hoist them up to the right height. A worker then guides them to their respective positions. This last task is the responsibility of carpenters and fitters, many of whom previously worked on large viaducts, and even some boatswains who have traded the open sea for the open sky. Regardless of their training, they are all true acrobats. Once the pieces are in position, they are assembled using cone-shaped pins that are hammered in using a mallet, followed by temporary bolts.

Once this is done, the riveters take over. There are initially four teams per pillar and then only two upon reaching the second floor. Each of the four team members has a clear role: one man heats the rivet red-hot, the second man inserts it into the appropriate hole and holds it in place by the head that has already been formed, the third man strikes the metal from the other side to form the second head, and the final man beats it with a sledgehammer. When they cool down, the rivets contract and hold the parts firmly together. These teams of flying blacksmiths fit approximately one hundred rivets per day in a noisy cloud of smoke.

Gustave Eiffel on site with his workforce
at the foundation-laying stage.

EXTREME CONDITIONS

On the morning of September 19, 1888, only 27 of the expected 140 workers show up at the work site. The others are on strike. Once the structure reaches the second floor, these acrobats no longer feel that their pay is sufficient. The pay may be better on the Tower work site than elsewhere, but the working conditions are harsh: they work in the open air, hundreds of feet above the ground, and risk falling at every turn. Not only that, but the work days are long: twelve-hour days during scorching summer months (temperatures in Paris climb to over 100 °F in August 1888) and nine-hour days during especially harsh winters (temperatures as low as 10 °F in 1889).

Even the slightest delay could compromise their strict timeline and Eiffel grants the workers the requested raise. However, when conflict breaks out again in December, he will simply sideline the strike leaders. That being said, Eiffel is not a bad boss. He is aware of the difficulties his workers face and funds canteens on the structure's first floor and then on the second floor. He also promises bonuses. As for the men who supervise the on-site workers over the twenty-six months, they are all expert veterans who are intimately familiar with colossal projects. The site foreman, Jean Compagnon, is one of Eiffel's right-hand men. He worked with Eiffel on the construction of numerous structures, such as the Garabit viaduct and the Maria Pia bridge in Portugal. He is seconded by Eugène Milon, another experienced company man and part of Eiffel's inner circle.

Using a hydraulic jack, workers quite literally raise up one
of the Tower's supports to slip in a wedge.

THE TOWER
SYMBOL OF THE "IRON AGE"

The Eiffel Tower isn't the first metal structure to be built in France's capital. Since the beginning of the century, train station canopies, the covered walkways of the *Grands Boulevards*, the *Halles de Baltard*, and the greenhouses in the *Jardin des plantes* have accustomed Parisians to this new kind of architecture. But this innovative material – which is sturdier, lighter, and easier to use – has never been presented to them so majestically and unapologetically.

The Tower will become the resounding symbol of the transition from the "Stone Age" to the "Iron Age." And not just any iron… Like on all of his work sites, Eiffel uses puddle iron, invented by the Englishman Henry Cort in 1784. Puddling is a process that involves stirring the liquid iron, resulting in an iron that is low in carbon and thus less prone to corrosion. Considering the fact that Eiffel plans to expose more than 11,000 tons of iron to the wind and the elements, this detail is anything but insignificant. Eiffel therefore calls upon a company that he has worked with before: the Fould-Dupont foundry and factory in Pompey, near Nancy. The ore itself comes from mines in Lorraine. In essence, the Tower's iron is 100% French.

At first-floor level, in letters of gold, Gustave Eiffel had inscribed the names of 72 intellectuals who had made a contribution to France in the period 1789-1889.

Emblematic examples of 20th Century ironwork: above, Paris's elevated metro railway, pictured in 1980; opposite page, a covered walkway in Vichy Park at the turn of the century.

GOING UP
THE TOWER

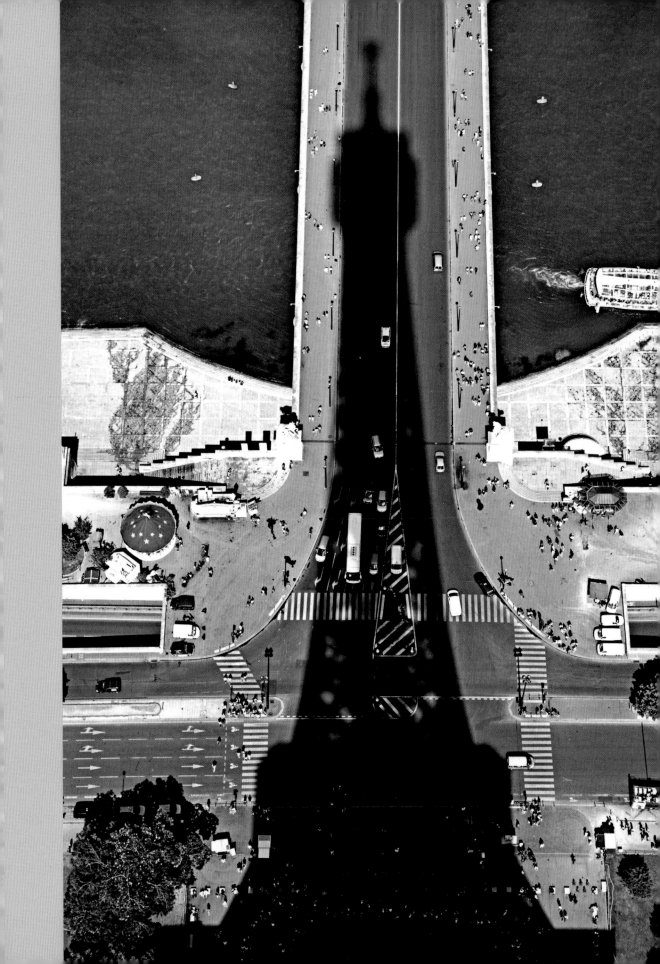

WINNING VISITORS FOR THE IRON LADY

With its inauguration on March 31, 1889, the Eiffel Tower embarks on a new adventure. Over the past two years, the work site has become a veritable attraction for all of Paris, but the Iron Lady must now become a monument in her own right. It needs to be an attraction for people to visit, a destination for outings for the family or friends, something to show family members from out of town, a place to admire the panorama of the city and the virtuosity of contemporary engineering. Eiffel knows that there is no way around it: the Tower must attract visitors!

After all, its financial survival depends on it. The engineer from Burgundy may have demonstrated his technical and industrial expertise by raising 11,000 tons of iron up to 984 feet above the ground, but now he must prove his economic and financial ingenuity. On January 8, 1887, when he signed the contract binding him to the State and the city, he took a major risk, but also gave birth to one of the first – and undoubtedly one of the most famous – public-private partnerships in the world.

As is the case for certain highways or railways today, the agreement stipulated that Gustave Eiffel should finance the construction of the monument himself (although the State does grant him 1.5 million francs – a little over 6 million euros today and approximately 20% of the estimated total cost). In exchange, he will enjoy "the Tower's exploitation rights" for twenty years after the closing of the Exhibition, at which point the Tower will become the property of Paris. To sum up, Eiffel will only manage to cover his costs if visitors flock to the Tower.

OPPOSITE
Once building is complete, the Tower quickly becomes one of Paris's most emblematic monuments.

It's quite a gamble, but it will quickly pay off for the entrepreneur and his associates (a consortium of banks made up of the *Société Générale*, the *Banque franco-égyptienne*, and the *Crédit industriel et commercial*). During the 1889 Universal Exhibition, more than two million visitors rush to climb the Tower and enjoy its kiosks, restaurants, and shops. After the first year, the work site costs are covered and the Eiffel Tower becomes profitable. This is still the case today: the Tower is one of the very rare French monuments not to receive any public funding.

Then again, Gustave Eiffel plays his hand remarkably well. In terms of publicity and the media, his Tower benefits from unprecedented and continuous hype thanks to the ongoing protests it inspires. Keenly aware of the inner workings of the press, Eiffel even installs a Figaro newspaper print shop on the second floor of the monument. The Tower is already a star before its grand opening. Of course, once Eiffel has his hordes of eager visitors, he needs a way to get them to the top.

Yet again, Gustave Eiffel displays his technical prowess. Elevators of that height have never been built before! Likewise, elevators have never transported so many people and so quickly! The invention itself has only been around for about fifty years. The world's first real public elevator was installed in 1857 in a store in New York… But the Tower will have five (two connecting the ground level and the first floor, two running from the ground level to the second floor, and one more from the second floor's platform to the third floor). Considering the shape of the structure and Eiffel's strict requirements regarding comfort and safety, new technical solutions will be necessary. After calling upon all available technical resources to erect the tallest structure ever built, Eiffel must now turn it into a veritable machine to thrill the crowds.

15 cent. le numéro.

LE PETIT

5e Année. — N° 42

MONITEUR ILLUSTRÉ

GRAVURES. — **UN VOYAGE A LA TOUR EIFFEL** : — AU PIED DE LA TOUR. — LES ABORDS DU PILIER EST. — A LA PREMIÈRE PLATE-FORME. — SUR LA PREMIÈRE GALERIE. — L'ASCENSEUR DES PROVISIONS. — DANS L'ESCALIER. — OUF ! — AUTOUR DE L'ASCENSEUR DE LA TROISIÈME PLATE-FORME. — COUPE DE LA PARTIE SUPÉRIEURE DE LA TOUR. — LA DESCENTE. — MUSIQUE : *Mazurka* de Chopin.

DIMANCHE 20 OCTOBRE 1889

Six mois : **4** fr. — Un an : **8** fr.

On s'abonne sans frais dans tous les bureaux de poste.
PARIS. — 13, QUAI VOLTAIRE. — PARIS.

TEXTE. — **UN VOYAGE A LA TOUR EIFFEL**, par G. Lenôtre. — LE CAPITAINE FRACASSE, roman par Théophile Gautier. — LA VEUVE AU BOIS DORMANT, roman par Gustave Claudin. — MOSAÏQUE, par un Liseur. — LES LIEUTENANTS DU 25e, roman par Mme Louise Gérald. — RÉCRÉATIONS DE LA FAMILLE.

UN VOYAGE A LA TOUR EIFFEL. — A la première plate-forme.

CE NUMÉRO EST CONSACRÉ A LA TOUR EIFFEL.

No one had ever seen Paris from such a height. The exterior gallery on the second floor becomes one of the most sought-after viewpoints in the capital.

1

2

3

From the outset, Gustave Eiffel wanted to give the monument lasting appeal as a genuine tourist attraction. With this in mind, he installs restaurants, tea rooms and even a post office from which visitors can send postcards on sale in the numerous souvenir shops.

1. Menu for Thursday 18 July 1889, in the restaurant Le Brébant de la Tour.

2. Souvenir shop on the first floor.

3. Restaurant dining room, pictured around 1900.

4. Two visitors to the Eiffel Tower (photograph on painted background).

5. The highest mailbox in Paris (pictured in the 1930s).

4

5

ELEVATORS OF A UNIQUE KIND

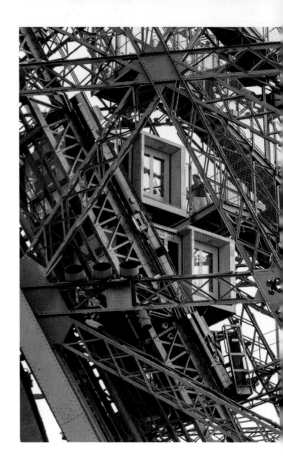

Elevator technology was still in its infancy and installing elevators in the Eiffel Tower will be yet another technical exploit. First of all, nobody has ever attempted lifting so much weight so high. Secondly, the curvature of the pillars between the ground and the second floor necessitates new solutions.

To solve this equation with several unknown variables, Eiffel calls upon several different companies. In the North and South pillars, the American company Otis installs a two-level cabin that can transport fifty passengers directly to the second floor. For the East and West pillars, Eiffel tasks the French company Roux, Combaluzier et Lepape with bringing visitors to the first floor and its restaurants, brasseries and shops. These two elevators are able to transport 100 people per trip and can make ten trips per hour. Last but not least, the Edoux company invents a one-of-a-kind hydraulic machine to reach the third floor. As the upper cabin is pushed upward by a 266-foot hydraulic ram, the lower cabin acts as a counterweight. The system requires passengers to change cabins half-way through, but the breathtaking view from the intermediate platform largely outweighs this minor inconvenience.

THE TOWER, ON THE CUTTING EDGE OF ENERGY RECOVERY

In 1887, when construction on the Eiffel Tower begins, electricity is still in its infancy and energy is both rare and expensive. To save on costs, the elevator designers invent a system of energy recovery generated by the cabin's descent. The same principle will later be applied to Formula 1 cars and classic automobiles with energy recovery generated by braking, for example. Today, the Tower's elevators still operate this way. Thanks to their continued renovation and recent technological advances, this system has been further improved and their electric power has been reduced by a quarter.

RIGHT HAND PAGE
On the walkway at first-floor level, smart travelers switch elevators to reach the top. Period of the 1900 Universal Exhibition.

The first principle of architectural esthetics is that a monument's fundamental lines should be determined by the perfect appropriation of its intended function. And what was the primary condition that dictated my conception of the Tower? Wind resistance. I maintain, therefore, that the mathematically determined curvature of the monument's framework, which starts out uncommonly wide at the base and tapers off as it nears the top, will create an impression of strength and beauty. After all, the colossal has a certain attraction and charm to which theories of the ordinary arts are scarcely applicable.

Gustave Eiffel, *Le Monde*, 1887

KILOMETERS (64,000 MILES) ARE COVERED EACH YEAR BY THE EIFFEL TOWER'S ELEVATORS – THAT IS TO SAY, TWO AND HALF TIMES AROUND THE EARTH

The Tower's "historic" elevators are carefully maintained and regularly renovated.
They have been in service now for more than a century.
Pictured above in 1954, and opposite in 2018.

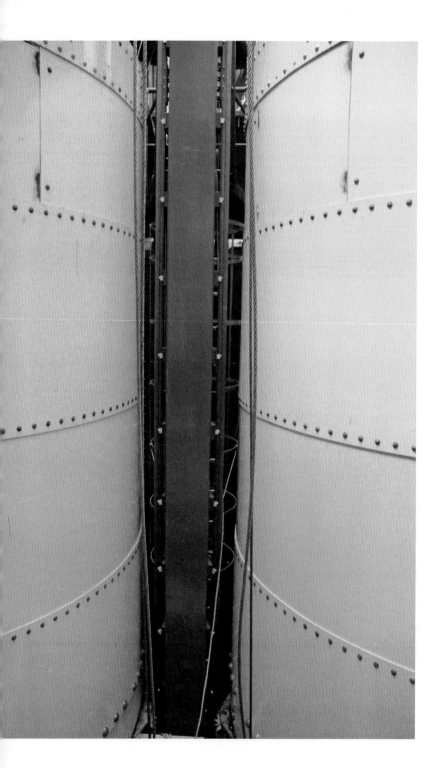

"HISTORIC" MACHINES MORE THAN ONE HUNDRED YEARS OLD

While the Edoux elevator from the second to the third floor would remain in service until 1983, the lifespan of the others would be much shorter due to technological advances. In 1910, the Otis elevators were dismantled and replaced, and have continued to be regularly replaced ever since. Eleven years earlier, the unreliable Roux, Combaluzier et Lepape machines had been changed out for elevators created by the Fives-Lille company with an unrivaled reputation in mechanics. These legendary yellow cabins, which have been regularly updated and still operate to this day, are carried by an underground cart that is powered by pistons activated by high pressure oil hydraulic motors. These monuments within the monument continue to be carefully maintained by a team of approximately fifty technicians.

OPPOSITE
The comfort of visitors comes before all else! There's a seat for everyone in these Otis elevators. Gravure by Poyet, 1889.

ABOVE
Close-up view of original hydraulic accumulators.

PRECARIOUS STAIRWAYS

"We followed Mr. Eiffel and our guide in single file to the right pillar where the staircase began. (...) Mr. Eiffel advised me to imitate him. He climbed the steps very slowly with his right arm on the ramp and rocked his body from one leg to the other. He used this momentum to climb each step. At that point, the incline was such that we could talk as we climbed and nobody was out of breath upon reaching the landing on the first floor."

In *Le Petit Moniteur Illustré* on March 17, 1889, the journalist Hugues Le Roux describes his first trip up the stairs of the Eiffel Tower, which is still in progress. He has just climbed 360 steps to reach the first floor and is hardly out of breath. There are 380 more steps separating him from the second floor, but this time, talking is not an option. The second spiral staircase (without any intermediate landings) turns out to be much steeper than the first. And as for the third, as the visitor climbs each of the 1,062 spiral steps, only a thin guardrail separates him from the void. This third and dizzying staircase will soon be closed to the public.

Take the elevator or climb the stairs? For visitors to the Universal Exhibition of 1900,
there might be problems with either choice.

>>

Visitors climb the Tower by means of stairways and an ingenious combination of elevators, as described in Attachment 2. The Eiffel Tower will undoubtedly enjoy the success it merits and we hope that it will also prove useful for scientific experiments, which would be interesting to carry out at such a height. Moreover, the Tower will become the property of the City once the twenty-year concession granted to Mr. Eiffel for the land it occupies has expired.

Paris city council report, 1889

1802

THE NUMBER OF STEPS FROM THE ESPLANADE TO THE TOP TAKING THE EAST PILLAR STAIRCASE: 360 STEPS FROM THE ESPLANADE TO THE FIRST FLOOR, 380 FROM THE FIRST FLOOR TO THE SECOND FLOOR, AND 1062 BETWEEN THE SECOND AND THIRD FLOORS

OFFERT PAR LA TOUR EIFFEL AU
MUSEE NATIONAL DES SCIENCES DES
TECHNIQUES ET DES INDUSTRIES
LE 29 JUIN 1983

ESCALIER D'ORIGINE
TOUR EIFFEL
– 1889 –

SALE AS SEPARATE LOTS

In 1983, the breathtaking staircase connecting the second and third floors is dismantled and cut into twenty-four sections measuring seven to thirty feet in length. These pieces of the Tower are immediately collector's items and the subject of heated bidding. Although two of the pieces may still be viewed by the public (in the Tower and at the History of Iron Musem in Nancy), most of the others are now part of private collections.

169 000

EUROS. THE SUM THAT A COLLECTOR FROM THE MIDDLE EAST SPENT ON TWENTY-FIVE STEPS FROM THE EIFFEL TOWER'S STAIRCASE IN NOVEMBER 2018. A LITTLE OVER 6,700 EUROS PER STEP...

OPPOSITE
A display of pride.
In 1889, Gustave Eiffel poses at the top of the Tower with his son-in-law and collaborator M. Salles.

et son Gendre et collaborateur M. Salles
Mr G. Eiffel au sommet de la Tour   ND. Phot

ESTABLISHING A FUTURE FOR THE TOWER

MAKING
THE TOWER
NECESSARY AND
PERMANENT

One hundred and thirty years after its creation, the Eiffel Tower has become one of the most visited and photographed monuments in the world, the irreplaceable emblem of Paris itself. For visitors today, it's impossible to imagine the French capital without the Tower's slender and elegant silhouette. And yet...

In 1909, twenty years after its inauguration, its demise was a very real subject of conversation. On 31 December, the exploitation rights granted to Gustave Eiffel expired and ownership of the monument transferred to the city of Paris. What to do? Should they destroy it as they had initially planned? After all, that was the fate of other structures built for the Universal Exhibitions of 1889 and 1900. The argument gains ground. Besides, after attracting huge crowds in its first years, the number of visitors has decreased at a dizzying rate. During the Exhibition in 1900, hardly more than a million people attempted the climb – half as many as eleven years earlier. Even worse, between 1901 and 1909, the number of tickets sold per year only exceeded 190,000 once – and not by much. To sum up, the Tower is out of date, just like iron architecture in general. With the emergence of Art Nouveau, stonework is in vogue once again, especially the recently "reinvented" reinforced concrete.

Obsolete and almost anachronistic, the Iron Lady owes her survival in large part to the man who created her. Having undoubtedly anticipated the threats against his masterpiece, Gustave Eiffel has continuously encouraged its use for scientific experimentation in optics, meteorology, communications, aerodynamics, etc. The attentive engineer ensures that everything related

to modern technological innovations has its place at the Tower. Therein lies the major argument for its conservation: this "gigantic factory chimney" (as some critics continued to call it) may not please everyone esthetically, but it is useful. It soon even receives the support of the "French Association for Scientific Advancement" and the "Society of Civil Engineers" as the debate rages on from 1900 to 1910. In a report submitted to the Prefect of the Seine's administrative department, the architect Jean-Louis Pascal sums up the situation: "Considering the value of a construction that is, after all, unique in the world (…), the fact that it continues to be a source of curiosity for visitors (…), and above all, this structure's exceptional adaptation for past, present, and future scientific research (…), would we sacrifice all of that for a harsh esthetic assessment and destroy at perhaps great cost (…) a monstrous building (…) simply because we'd like it to be more beautiful?"

The answer is "no". In 1910, the Tower is definitively saved and the concession is extended. This is excellent news for meteorological science, wireless telegraphy, the radio, and later television. The 984-foot-tall Tower will enable them to make undeniable progress. The French army will also use it to their advantage. By guiding airplanes and intercepting enemy radio communications, the Iron Lady

will become one of the little-known soldiers of the Great War. Paris can finally breathe a sigh of relief. The Tower, *their* Tower, will forever be part of the capital's skyline. This longevity will require numerous and ongoing adjustments. Every seven years, for example, a new layer of paint is necessary to protect it from the bite of the passing years. More occasionally, resourceful light tailors are called upon to mend the Iron Lady's twinkling gown. A series of more or less regular in-depth renovations is ongoing. In 1937, 1982, 2011, and more recently, since 2018, the Tower has undergone major restoration work. Thanks to these makeovers, it continues to be forever contemporary and the very image of modernity, even 130 years later.

OPPOSITE
Every seven years
for the past 130 years,
our beautiful Parisienne's
looks are restored
with a fresh coat of paint,
as here in 1924.

EIFFEL AT WORK

A visionary entrepreneur and peerless organizer, Eiffel is above all an engineer with a passion for technological progress and scientific experimentation. He will be able to give free rein to these pursuits starting in 1893 when his reputation is unfairly tarnished by the Panama Scandal that shakes the Republic to its core. He decides to withdraw from the business scene and dedicate himself fully to research. To this end, the Eiffel Tower will serve as a veritable laboratory.

Already equipped with a meteorological observation station, the Tower will soon boast numerous other instruments: barometers, anemometers, lightning rods, a Foucault pendulum, etc. The Tower thus becomes a research site for atmospheric pressure and temperature, wind speed and its effects on structures, objects' resistance to the open air, the effects of altitude on human physiology, and the list goes on.

In 1909, Eiffel even installs a small wind tunnel at the base of the monument in which he will carry out nearly 5,000 experiments. The ancestor of many large wind tunnels to come, this innovation makes him one of the world's pioneers in aerodynamics.

La Science Jllustrée

JOURNAL HEBDOMADAIRE

Publié sous la Direction de **Louis Figuier**

175395

Prix du Numéro:

25 CENTIMES.

6.ᶠ Le Volume Semestriel.

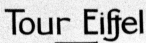

Tour Eiffel

Anémomètre électromagnétique Papillon
Vitesse instantanée
du vent en mètres/seconde
Moulinet Robinson à 4 Coupes, diamètre total : 0"225

Altitude : au-dessus du sol : 305"
au-dessus du niveau de la mer : 338"5

20

YEARS. THE TOWER'S INTENDED LIFESPAN.
IT WAS SAVED BY THE SCIENTIFIC
EXPERIMENTS THAT EIFFEL ENCOURAGED
AND IN PARTICULAR, THE FIRST
RADIO TRANSMISSIONS FOLLOWED
BY TELECOMMUNICATIONS

ABOVE
On 29 July 1898, France's first-ever wireless telegraph messages
are broadcast between the Eiffel Tower and the Panthéon.

WHEN THE TOWER BECAME A SOLDIER

Despite all of Eiffel's efforts, the Tower will ultimately be saved by an outside invention: wireless transmission. In November 1898, the Tower is the site of the first wireless telegraphy trials in France as the scientist Eugène Ducretet manages to send a message to the Panthéon, 2.5 miles from the Champ-de-Mars. Five years later, Eiffel authorizes Captain Gustave Ferrié to use the Tower to test military applications of this new technology. Even better, he finances the installation of the antennas himself…

France is indebted to him yet again. During the Great War, the Tower is requisitioned for its strategic value. Over the next four years, the Iron Lady will intercept many crucial messages enabling the French to repel German forces in 1914 during the Battle of the Marne, for example, or to unmask the famous spy Mata Hari. Less active during World War II, the Tower will nonetheless serve as a symbol of the Resistance. Cleverly sabotaged by its employees, the monument's elevators will be at a standstill throughout the Occupation.

The Eiffel Tower was requisitioned in the Great War and would play an important role
in the defeat of Germany, thanks to wireless transmission.

LES VINGT-CINQ ANS DE LA TOUR EIFFEL

Son utilisation actuelle pour la télégraphie sans fil

Wireless transmission, radio and television broadcasting: the Eiffel Tower would have a role
to play in every great technological innovation of the 20th Century.

324

METERS (1,063 FEET). THE CURRENT HEIGHT, INCLUDING THE 120 ANTENNAS

THE MOTHER OF THE RADIO...

After wireless transmission, the Tower contributes to another major innovation in telecommunications: the radio. In 1921, a civilian transmitter is installed that broadcasts music and programs a few hours per day. In 1925, the first "spoken news" in the world is broadcast from the Tower. Yet another first...

...AND FRENCH TELEVISION

After the radio, the Eiffel Tower witnesses the early years of television in the 1930s, but this new media won't inexorably take off until after World War II. This development will also usher in changes for the Tower. Several improvements in technology and new antennas later, the Tower climbs to new heights: 1043 feet in 1957 and 1063 feet in 2000.

LEFT
Special edition of *L'Illustration* featuring wireless transmission, 3 March 1923.

ONGOING RENOVATIONS

The latest round of renovations began in 2017 and will end in 2024. Thanks to a three hundred million euro budget (230 million from the SETE and 70 million from the city of Paris), the Iron Lady will get a new lease of life. This head to toe makeover includes the beacon at the very top of the Tower, a new layout for the gardens at her feet, a change in décor on the second floor, and the construction of a glass wall near the pillars, not to mention paint and lighting. Then again, over the course of her 130 years and many generations of workers, the Iron Lady should be accustomed to people bustling around her girders. Her first major renovation dates back to 1900 when, for the new Universal Exhibition, Eiffel decided to make his Tower more modern and welcoming by improving the machinery, the elevators, and the lighting as well as completely reorganizing the three floors. In 1937, another Exhibition contributed its share of changes. After that, the Tower would have to wait until 1982 for its next complete overhaul. More renovations in 2011 and 2017 would further contribute to the Tower's radiant modernity.

1343

METRIC TONS (1,480 TONS). THE WEIGHT THAT THE TOWER SHED DURING THE RENOVATION WORK IN 1982 BY DISMANTLING A CONCRETE SLAB THAT HAD BEEN INSTALLED ON THE FIRST FLOOR IN 1937 AND REPLACING ITS STAIRCASES AND SOME OF THE ELEVATORS

THE COLORS
OF THE TOWER

Ever since the very beginning, the Tower's paint has played a critical role in maintaining and protecting its puddle iron from oxidation, pollution, and – on a less glamorous note – bird droppings. And from the very beginning, this legendary task has fallen to an army of painter-mountaineer acrobats who defy vertigo to repaint the whole structure manually using "scrub planes" (scrapers to scour the eroded paint) and brushes. This feat, which takes place every seven years, requires between 55 to 66 tons of paint and is an important event in the monument's life as it also represents the opportunity to check every square inch of the Tower and replace any corroded metal pieces. But there is much more to each painting campaign than just the technical aspects. Symbolically, the paint also dresses the Iron Lady in a gown that has changed in color over the years from various red, yellow, and ocher hues to its current "Eiffel Tower Brown." This unique color is also an important part of the Tower's identity.

7

**THE AVERAGE NUMBER
OF YEARS BETWEEN EACH
PAINTING CAMPAIGN**

A MORE ECOLOGICALLY FRIENDLY PAINT!

Ever since the 2002 campaign, the SETE has paid particular attention to the composition of the paint used. After replacing lead pigments with zinc phosphate, the SETE went on to eliminate almost all solvents. The Tower is now more environmentally friendly and more resistant to corrosion.

OPPOSITE
Painter balancing on
an Eiffel Tower staircase,
September 1907.

2,5

MILLION SQUARE METERS (26,909,776 SQUARE FEET). THE PAINTER-MOUNTAINEERS MUST PAINT THE ENTIRE STRUCTURE, GIRDER AFTER GIRDER AND RIVET AFTER RIVET DURING EACH PAINTING CAMPAIGN – THE EQUIVALENT OF MORE THAN 40 TIMES THE TOTAL SURFACE AREA OF THE VERSAILLES CHÂTEAU!

ABOVE
Scientific experiment on the Eiffel Tower, 1921.

COLORS OF THE EIFFEL TOWER
ACROSS THE YEARS

1887

A MINIMUM "VENETIAN RED" PAINT
IS APPLIED IN THE LEVALLOIS
WORKSHOP BEFORE THE PARTS
ARE SENT OFF TO THE CHAMP-
DE-MARS FOR ASSEMBLY

1889

JUST BEFORE THE INAUGURATION,
EIFFEL'S PAINTER, MR. NOURRISSON,
HAS A LAYER OF LINSEED OIL
APPLIED FOLLOWED BY A SHINY
AND VERY THICK REDDISH-
BROWN COAT

1892

THE TOWER BECOMES
"OCHER-BROWN"

1899

THE TOWER IS PAINTED IN FIVE
GRADUATED COLORS, FROM
YELLOW-ORANGE AT THE BASE
TO LIGHT YELLOW AT THE TOP.
AFTER THIS REPAINTING
CAMPAIGN, THE SEVEN-YEAR
CYCLE IS ADOPTED

1907

THE COLOR USED IS NOW CALLED
"YELLOW-BROWN"

1954

THE EIFFEL TOWER'S COLOR
CHANGES TO "RED-BROWN"

1968

THE "EIFFEL TOWER BROWN" COLOR
IS SELECTED BECAUSE IT WORKS
WELL WITH THE PARIS CITYSCAPE.
THE COLOR IS GRADUATED IN THREE
TONES, FROM THE DARKEST AT THE
BOTTOM TO THE LIGHTEST AT THE TOP

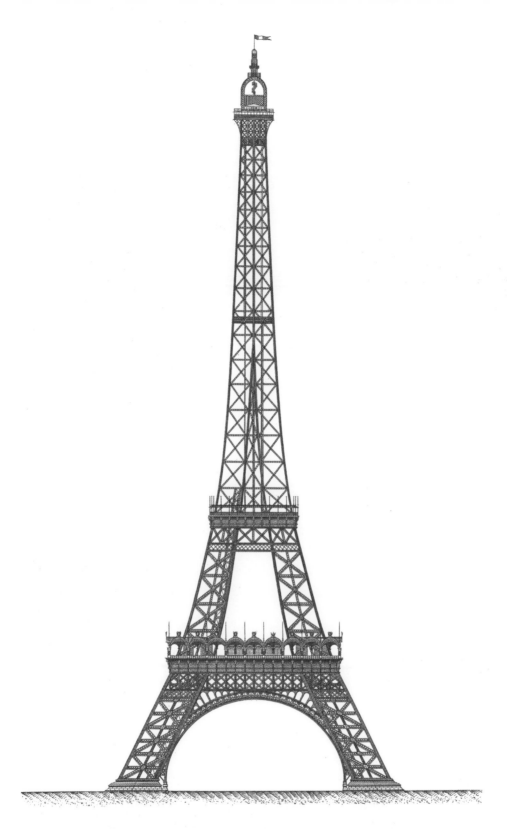

2019

THE TOWER RETURNS TO ITS 1907 COLOR

LIT
BY NIGHT

Ever since the turn of
the millennium, as soon as
evening falls, 20,000 lights
(5,000 per side of the Tower's
structure) sparkle in the
capital's sky for five minutes
at the beginning of each hour.

An Iron Lady living in the City of Lights… Ever since its birth, the Eiffel Tower's silhouette has featured remarkable lighting that accentuates its grace and presence every evening after nightfall. Always on the cutting edge of technology, the Tower has born witness to the technological evolutions in lighting over the past 130 years.

For its inauguration in 1889, an electric beacon at the top of the Tower (which was considered to be the most powerful in the world) could light up to 62 miles in any direction. Ten thousand gaslights completed the effect. However, thanks to technological progress, these lights were replaced by five thousand incandescent bulbs, which were placed along the Tower's framework and decorative arches in 1900. Fluorescent lights and high-pressure sodium lamps would follow, and it is these that have given the Tower its beautiful golden color ever since 1985.

20 000

**THE NUMBER OF LIGHT BULBS
THAT MAKE THE TOWER SPARKLE
EACH NIGHT**

What better choice than a Parisian icon to publicize your brand?
In the 1920s, the Citröen company would use the Tower to display its name in lights on a grand scale.

A glance, an object, a symbol, the Tower is everything that man makes her, and that everything is infinite. A spectacle to be looked at which returns your gaze, at once useless and irreplaceable, a familiar sight and heroic symbol, the witness of a century and yet always new, inimitable and yet constantly reproduced: it is a pure sign and an unbridled metaphor, open to all times, to all images, and to all meanings. The Tower prompts men to exercise that great faculty that is the imagination, and they are free to do so, for no history – however dark – has ever managed to take that away from them.

Roland Barthes and André Martin, *La Tour Eiffel*, Lausanne, Delpire, 1964

300

KILOMETERS (186 MILES). THE RANGE OF
THE TWO PROJECTORS INSTALLED AT THE TOP
OF THE EIFFEL TOWER IN 1947 IN ORDER
TO ASSIST AIRCRAFT NAVIGATION. THESE
WERE DAMAGED AND TAKEN DOWN IN 1974.
HOWEVER, ON DECEMBER 31, 1999,
TO CELEBRATE THE NEW MILLENNIUM,
A NEW (AND LESS POWERFUL) BEACON
WAS INSTALLED THAT CONTINUES
TO SWEEP THE PARIS NIGHT SKY

THE EIFFEL TOWER

UNIVERSAL ICON

BY BENJAMIN PEYREL

Éditions
de La Martinière

ABRAMS | NEW YORK

Original text (French): Benjamin Peyrel
Translation from French: Anna Howell
Editor and Picture Research: Laetitia Réal-Moretto
Design and graphic production: Élisabeth Welter

With the collaboration of

SOCIETE D'EXPLOITATION DE LA TOUR EIFFEL

Distributed in 2020 by Abrams, an imprint of ABRAMS
Copyright © 2019 Éditions de La Martinière, an imprint of
EDLM, for the French original edition and English translation.

Photoengraving: Studio 4c
Printed and bound in August 2019 by Pollina, France - 90637
ISBN : 978-1-4197-4429-7

Abrams® is a registered trademark of Harry N. Abrams, Inc.

ABRAMS The Art of Books
195 Broadway, New York, NY 10007
abramsbooks.com

CONTENTS

UNIVERSAL SYMBOL OF THE CITY OF LIGHTS

"I love the Paris of great minds – a Paris that is threatened by this truly tragic street lamp which springs forth from her belly and will be visible by night twenty leagues above the mountaintops, like a beacon of disaster and despair."

Léon Bloy may have been known for dipping his quill in acid more often than ink, but his biting and caustic wit doesn't exclude a certain level of lucid and visionary thinking. A few lines later, in this collection of texts written between 1884 and 1900, he adds:

"I APPEAL, HOWEVER, TO ITS CONSTRUCTION
WITH ALL MY BEING [...] BECAUSE I SENSE THAT
THIS FINE METAL TRINKET HAS QUITE
THE FUTURE IN STORE."[1]

And what a future! One hundred and thirty years after its birth, Huysmans' "hollow candlestick" or Maupassant's "disgraceful giant skeleton" has not only become one of the most visited entrance-fee monuments in the world (more than 300 million people have taken in its breathtaking views), but it has also become a piece of art in its own right.

Initially celebrated as a scientific and technical feat, the Tower is now the object of enthusiastic praise for its grace, its lightness, and its eternal modernity. The crowning monument of a Universal Exhibition has become an icon, synonymous with France and her capital city. In a poll carried out in 1987, one quarter of the French considered it to be...

1 Léon Bloy, *Belluaires et porchers*, Paris, Stock, 1905.

OPPOSITE
As a symbol of Paris and a universal icon, the Tower is seen in the company of the greatest stars, like Sarah Jessica Parker at the preview of the film *Sex and the City* in New York on 19 September 2007. *Tour d'Eiffel II* bag designed by Timmy Woods.

"THE PLACE OR MONUMENT THAT BEST SYMBOLIZES FRANCE."

Barely a hundred years after its birth, it had already ousted its illustrious ancestors (Versailles, the Arc de Triomphe, the Mont Saint-Michel) in the hearts of the French. As the philosopher Roland Barthes writes in 1964, "one might say that the Tower claimed its place from Paris itself, from its old stones and dense history. It conquered the old symbols just as it physically overshadows their domes and clock hands."[2] Perhaps even more impressive is the fact that this phenomenon extends beyond France's borders. In 2010, a major travel website surveyed 10,000 customers from all five continents to determine travelers' favorite monuments in the world: the Eiffel Tower came in at the top four, beating out St. Peter's in Rome, the Taj Mahal, and the Statue of Liberty.

Of course, before becoming the icon it is today in the eyes of the French and the rest of the world, Gustave Eiffel's tower had its fair share of challenges. After convincing France's authorities of its value and thereby saving it from destruction, the Tower then had to seduce a whole host of people, starting with artists and opinion makers, some of whom had violently protested its construction in the newspaper columns of the time. In the throes of a rekindled feud between supporters of the Old and the Modern, the Tower is tirelessly taunted and discredited by the former before being turned into a venerated site of worship by the latter. One of them, the Cubist precursor Robert Delaunay, uses colors and shapes to capture its dynamism on canvas.

THE SURREALISTS (AND ARAGON IN PARTICULAR) CELEBRATE THIS "TALL BLUE FEMALE" WHO IS "TENDER" AND, ABOVE ALL, "NEW." MEANWHILE, THE ART CRITIC FLORENT FELS DUBS THE TOWER "THE ULTIMATE SYMBOL OF A NEW ERA."

Thanks to these enlightened prophets, the Eiffel Tower is ushered into the avant-garde artistic world of the early 20th century. Little by little, this image makes its way across the rest of the world.

2 Roland Barthes and André Martin, *La Tour Eiffel*, Lausanne, Delpire, 1964.

OPPOSITE
Painter Robert Delaunay (1885-1941), one of the Tower's most fervent admirers, decorates it with colors that bring out the best in its exceptional lines.

In 1955, the famous architect Le Corbusier celebrates this new universal identity in his preface to a book entitled *La Tour Eiffel*, which was published that same year by Éditions de Minuit. "I bring to the Tower the testimony of a tireless pilgrim around the world. In the cities, in the savanna, in the pampas, in the desert, on the ghats, and on the estuaries, everywhere, in the hearts of the humble and the not-so-humble, the Tower is the symbol of a beloved Paris, a beloved symbol of Paris."[3]

GUSTAVE EIFFEL'S GIGANTIC IRON TOWER HAS GONE FAR BEYOND THE DREAMS OF ITS CREATOR AND ITS INITIAL FUNCTION; IT HAS CAPTURED THE WORLD'S IMAGINATION.

For its visitors, the vast majority of whom come from abroad, it embodies and showcases Paris itself and even France. When it dresses up in bright colors and fireworks for celebrations and commemorations or cloaks itself in darkness after tragic events, it becomes a universal symbol of liberty and solidarity for all citizens of the world. For artists and creative minds, the Iron Lady is a character in her own right: an actress in countless films, a model for millions of photos, the very embodiment of that inimitably chic Parisian woman's elegant silhouette, ready to "go for a jaunt" and "jump into the Seine feet first," as Charles Trenet used to sing …[4]

Léon Bloy was right. One hundred and thirty years after its birth, the Eiffel Tower has traded in the contempt and trends of the time for a dazzling destiny. This destiny continues thanks to hundreds of men and women who see to its upkeep, manage its perpetual renovations, constantly improve the visitors' experience, and further strengthen its image in France and abroad.

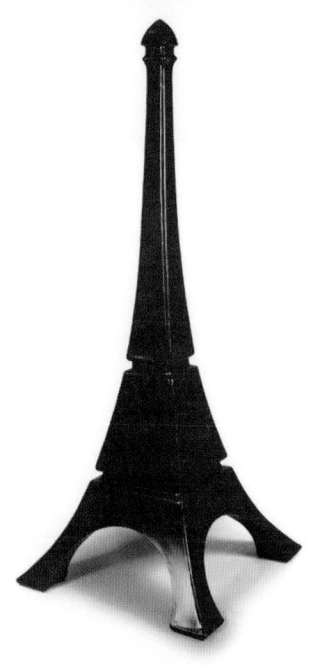

Designers, creatives, publicists …The Tower is an inspiration.

ABOVE
Design by
Arnaud Anseeuw.

OPPOSITE
Raymond Gid, for
Air France. "Fly to Paris,
Gateway to the World,"
1953.

3 Le Corbusier, preface to Charles Cordat, *La Tour Eiffel*, Paris, Éditions de Minuit, 1955.
4 Reference to Charles Trenet's song, "Y'a d'la joie."

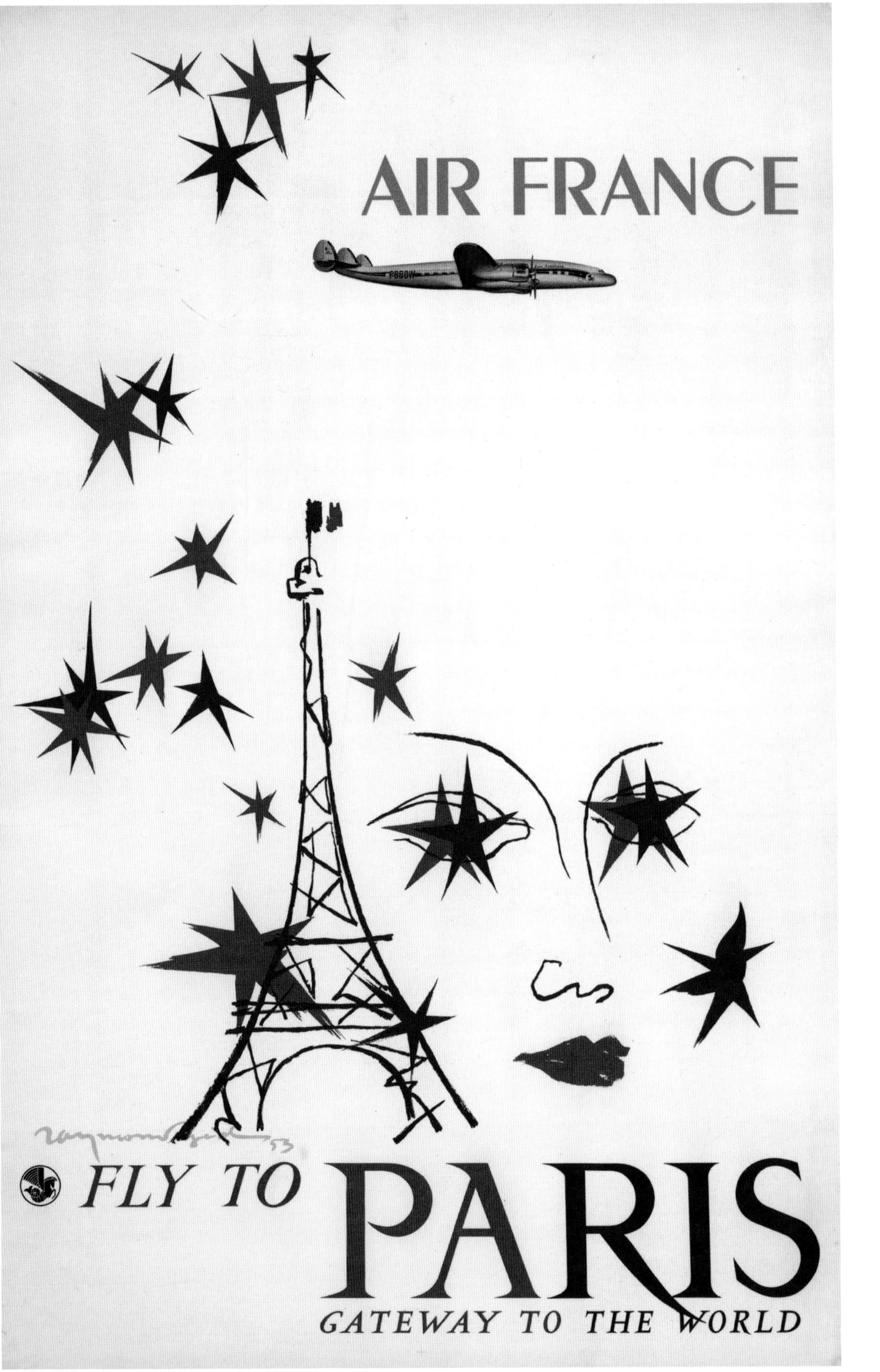

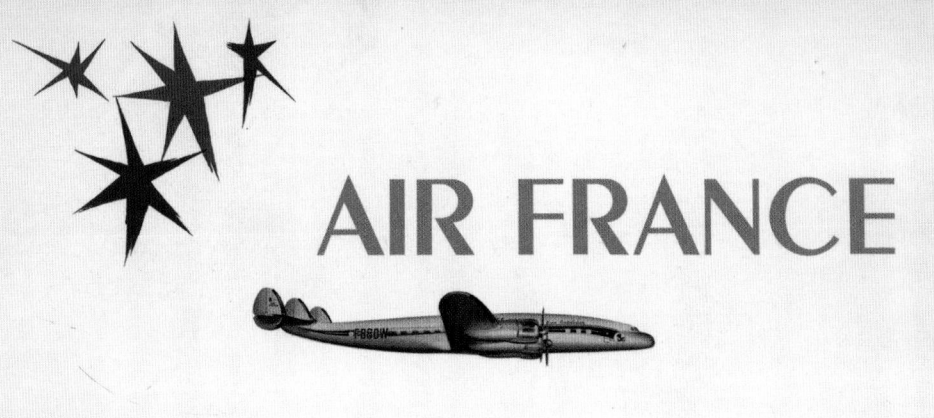

AIR FRANCE

FLY TO PARIS

GATEWAY TO THE WORLD

English students admire the view of the Champ-de-Mars and the Eiffel
Tower from the terrace of the Palais de Chaillot, in 1939.

THE SEDUCTRESS

THE MOST PARISIAN OF PARISIAN LADIES

"From that height, the tallest houses and people below looked tiny to me. This 300-meter tower, which is both delicate and solid in appearance, could never succumb to the ravages of time. It is truly the greatest and the most curious monument in the world."

While visiting Paris during the summer of 1896, Li Hongzhang, China's Ambassador Extraordinary, takes the opportunity to climb to the top of this new attraction that has the entire world buzzing. Back on solid ground, he leaves this eloquent comment in the monument's guest book. A little bit further down on the same page, El Maathi's signature is accompanied by even more enthusiastic praise. "The Eiffel Tower is the most marvelous thing that man has ever built," writes the head of the Moroccan embassy in France.

Gustave Eiffel may not have anticipated it, but his creation has turned out to be quite the seductress. Being attentive observers throughout the constructions process, Parisians quickly took it to their hearts. And as France's capital city has always set the tone regarding style and esthetics, the rest of the country followed suit and adopted this elegant symbol of French genius and greatness. Initially unmoved by her charms, artists also eventually succumbed, led by the avant-garde Cubists and Surrealists. Then people from all over the world fell head over heels for this proud, stately, and slender silhouette draped in iron lace with the same quintessential allure as those Parisian women that everybody so admires.

Forever young, forever new, the Tower continues to have the same effect on people 130 years after its

OPPOSITE
Chic, elegance and modernity ... these are the qualities that the Tower represents for great stylists like Balmain, in 1961.

16

birth. A glance at the visitors milling around the Tower's feet (80% of whom come from abroad) proves just how true that statement continues to be. With their craned necks, wide eyes, faces raised to the sky, and sometimes dumbstruck expressions, they praise the beauty of this modern Tower of Babel in all the languages of the world. One hundred and thirty years later, the magic is still very real.

One hundred and thirty years... Even the most coquette and narcissistic of starlets would never dare to dream of such a long career. Then again, the Iron Lady is careful to look after herself – or rather, others do so for her. Every day of the year, the teams of the SETE (*Société d'exploitation de la tour Eiffel*) work tirelessly to doll her up in beautiful and dazzling new gowns. In an effort to reinforce her appeal by day and by night and to keep her admirers on their toes, they constantly work to renovate, innovate, protect, and invent. In 2019, for example, all of the dining options – from the gastronomical "Jules Verne" restaurant to the take-away counters and the brasserie on the first floor – were revisited and entrusted to the Michelin-starred chefs Frédéric Anton and Thierry Marx. And every year, each season features new events and attractions so that no two visits are ever quite the same.

OPPOSITE PAGE
Couturiers certainly adore the Eiffel Tower. In 2019, the House of Saint-Laurent shows its collection at the Tower's feet.

ABOVE
Gastronomy at its highest with Thierry Marx and Frédéric Anton. The Tower has two Michelin-starred chefs to run its restaurants.

MILLION. THE AVERAGE NUMBER OF YEARLY VISITORS

From the date of its opening, the Tower has featured several restaurants that have changed with changing times and fashions. Seen here at the time of the Universal Exhibition, 1900.

FOLLOWING TWO PAGES
3D visualization of today's new brasserie on the first floor.

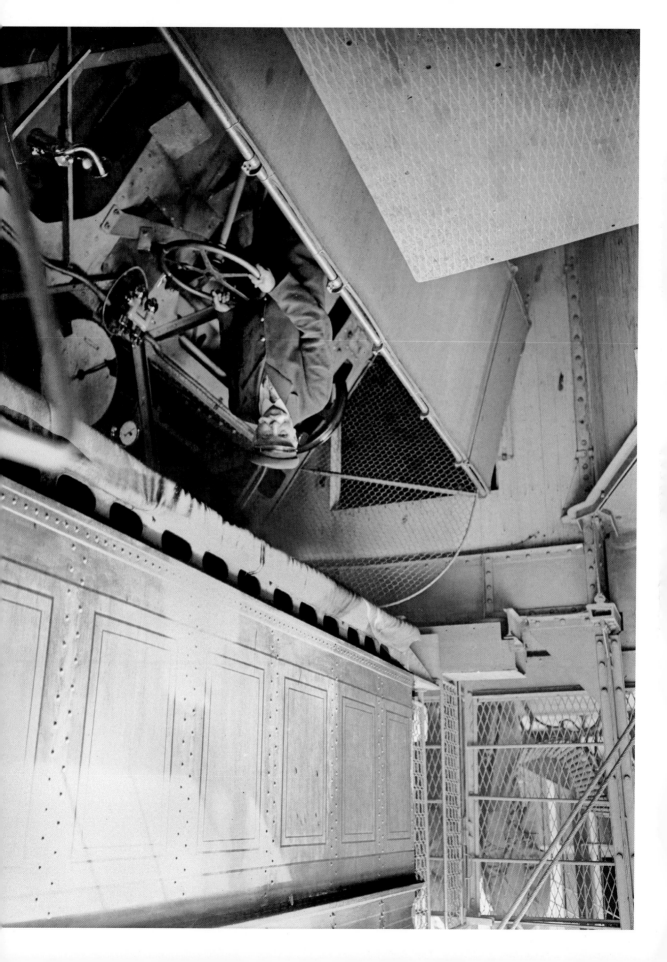

THE GUARDIANS OF A TIMELESS HERITAGE

The fact that the Eiffel Tower has managed to maintain its allure since its creation is partially thanks to the men and women who have carefully kept watch over it for the past 130 years. A bit of Eiffel's genius continues to inspire these painters, technicians, engineers, and creative minds to this day. Today, 700 passionate people dedicate their expertise to its continued success and an optimal experience for its 6 million yearly visitors. Nearly 350 of these individuals are employees of the SETE (*Société d'exploitation de la tour Eiffel*), the organism that the city of Paris has entrusted with managing and showcasing its patrimonial pride and joy. From the customer service and security staff members who receive visitors 365 days a year to the teams tasked with regularly brainstorming and organizing new events, or the numerous technicians responsible for the monument's maintenance, renovation work, and logistics, all of these individuals proudly contribute to making the French capital's crown jewel shine.

**THE APPROXIMATE NUMBER
OF NATIONALITIES REPRESENTED
BY THE SETE'S STAFF MEMBERS.
A RICHLY DIVERSE TEAM THAT REFLECTS
THE MONUMENT'S VISITORS**

OPPOSITE PAGE
Elevator driver
Basile Téron, pictured
around 1920.

Photos from the exhibition *Les Femmes et les Hommes de la Tour* (Women and Men of the Tower) shot by Karine Sicard Bouvatier to mark the 130th anniversary of the monument.

Nahema, Pascal, Régine, Julie, Jean-Philippe and Antoine (reception) – Gustave and Imed (security) – Georges (security), Bernard (presidency), Flore (sanitary maintenance), Christian (technical), Claudine (reception) and Patrick (directorate general) – Noura and Francelise (sanitary maintenance).

TOP TO BOTTOM AND LEFT TO RIGHT
André, Champagne Bar. Antonio, Hygiene. Nadia, Staff Restaurant..
Hervé and Antonio, Structural Maintenance.

Maybe one of the most photographed views in the world:
the Tower viewed from the Trocadéro esplanade.

CONSTANTLY RENEWED SUCCESS

300 million visitors! On September 28, 2018, one of the world's most visited entrance-fee monuments celebrates this symbolic milestone with fanfare: concerts on every floor, a special light show for the occasion, photos of Parisians and tourists on a 39-foot-long wall... However, this incredible success has been a long time in the making as the Tower's popularity has only shot up in the past fifty years. While it took the Tower 94 years to welcome its 100-millionth visitor in 1983, it only took nineteen years to double that number in 2002 and just fifteen more to reach the 300-million mark. This exponential increase is largely thanks to the explosion of mass tourism starting in the late-1960s, but is also thanks to the Tower's teams of workers who tirelessly renovate and innovate to renew the Eiffel Tower experience.

In 1937, Paris hosted a new International Exposition. And of course the Tower stood right
at the heart of the event, with the crowd gathered round.

Decades later, the Tower's powers of attraction are as strong as ever,
making it an essential feature of any Paris itinerary.

TIENES QUE IR A LA TORRE EIFFEL.
Es un lugar obligado cuando vas por Paris […]
Era mi tercera vez, pero como si fuera
la primera.

Rvaldivieson, Medellin, Colombia

A MUST. Dreams do come true.
I never imagined being able to see the Eiffel
Tower in person. It was magnificent.

Rosavlrl, Mission, Texas (United States)

MARCO DA CIDADE. É impossível não adorar
a Torre Eiffel. Passamos o dia a vê-la durante
os nossos passeios e quando chegamos perto
dela fica ainda mais bonita! Aconselho uma
visita de dia e outra de noite pois as luzes
piscam durante 10 minutos.

JessFreitas5, Lisbon, Portugal

WUNDERSCHÖN. Die Überschrift sagt alles.
Hammer Blick über die gesamte Stadt. [...]
Ein Traum! Ein wahres Meisterwerk!

OttfriedCB, Munich, Germany

LA TOUR EIFFEL, C'EST PARIS.
Venir ici sans aller la visiter, ce serait comme
ne pas être allé à Paris.

Olivia, Lyon, France

**THAT'S THE PROPORTION OF OVERSEAS
VISITORS AMONG THE 6 MILLION OR
SO WHO VISITED THE TOWER IN 2018**

Every year, the Eiffel Tower is the setting for the fireworks on 14 July,
in celebration of France's national day.

Famous actress Kim Novak (left, in 1959) and the equally famous Princess Margaret from England (right, in 1951).
A homage offered by one kind of celebrity to another.

VIP VISITORS

The list of the Tower's first official visitors features, among others, members of the royal families of England and Japan; the kings of Greece, Serbia, and Portugal; princes, princesses, and representatives of countries from all over the world; and even the famous cowboy Buffalo Bill whose "Wild West Show" at the Alma bridge racetrack captured Paris's imagination that spring of 1889. And while it's impossible to cite all of the sports and entertainment stars and all of the representatives of nations big and small who have since visited it, one thing is certain: the Eiffel Tower is a must-see when in Paris.

Tonight, dinner on the platform of the Eiffel Tower with the Charpentiers, Hermants, Zolas, and Dayots. We took the elevator up: a feeling akin to going out to sea, but not dizzying in the slightest. Up above, perception goes far beyond earthly thoughts, grandeur, the expanse, the Babylonian immensity that is Paris […] A somewhat dreamlike dinner… Followed by the peculiar sensation of the descent by foot, which was a little bit like diving headfirst into infinity.

Translation of an excerpt from Edmond and Jules de Goncourt's *Journal* (Tuesday, July 2, 1889)

Photographer André Kertész captures the tenderness of a couple
as they enjoy the Parisian panorama, in 1929.

PIONEER OF THE POSTCARD

Although the postcard was born in Austria in 1869, it wouldn't make its début in France until four years later. Either blank or decorated with advertising messages, it would only start to resemble the postcard as we know it today in August 1889 thanks to… the Eiffel Tower. The monument's success would give rise the first touristic postcard with an illustration on the left-hand side by the famous engraver Louis-Charles Libonis. This souvenir item for the 1889 Universal Exhibition would be so popular that it would continue to be sold long after the end of the Exhibition.

Nous n'avons vraiment pas le beau temps

2 PARIS
La Tour Eiffel

A PERPETUAL ATTRACTION

In the Paris of the early 20th century, the Eiffel Tower's very existence was a spectacle; it was new, surprising, inspiring. One hundred and thirty years later, famous throughout the world and looked upon daily by millions of tourists and Parisians, it continues to be a source of rejuvenation and surprise. Take, for example, the restaurants that have resided in the monument since its grand opening in 1889. At the time, there were four of them, in beautiful wooden pavilions designed by the architect Stephen Sauvestre. To keep up with the latest in gastronomy and tourism, the dining options have evolved over the years. In addition to the "on the go" buffets, the Tower is also home to two restaurants as well as champagne and macaron bars.

In order to ensure that no two visits are quite alike, the monument doesn't just depend on the weather or the changing Parisian cityscape. Each year, the SETE develops an extensive program of events. Depending on the seasons and other goings-on in Paris's social calendar, visitors have enjoyed skating and golfing on the first floor's platform, discovering exhibitions, participating in a historical escape game, and zooming high above the Champ-de-Mars on a thrilling zip-wire ride.

125

METERS (410 FEET). THE HEIGHT FROM WHICH THE EIFFEL TOWER OFFERS UP THE BEST IN FRENCH GASTRONOMY. EVER SINCE 1983, THE "JULES VERNE" RESTAURANT ON THE TOWER'S SECOND FLOOR HAS PROPOSED AN EXTRAORDINARY EXPERIENCE FOR CUSTOMERS' EYES AND TASTE BUDS ALIKE

Every age has its diversions. In 1900, the Tower itself
– along with several tourist stands – was pleasure enough for visitors.

One hundred and fifty years after the previous photo, novelties like this ice rink that was installed for a time at first floor level serve to ensure that no two visits are ever the same.

96%

ACCORDING TO A STUDY CARRIED
OUT IN 2017, 96% OF THIS EMBLEMATIC
MONUMENT'S VISITORS WOULD
RECOMMEND IT TO THEIR FRIENDS
AND FAMILY WHILE VISITING
THE FRENCH CAPITAL

A SOURCE
OF INSPIRATION

KNOWN ALL AROUND THE WORLD

It's a thrilling scene in a saga with its fair share of dramatic scenes. In *A View to a Kill*, Roger Moore (James Bond) chases Grace Jones (May Day) through the floors of the Eiffel Tower. When the elegant killer leaps into the air and gracefully floats down toward the Champ-de-Mars on a parachute, 007 attempts to catch up to her by jumping on top of one of the monument's elevators heading down…

Nearly thirty years earlier in 1956, the Iron Lady played opposite two other Hollywood stars as they danced across one of her platforms: Audrey Hepburn and Fred Astaire in Stanley Donen's *Funny Face*. More recently, in 2017, the first floor set the scene for a wedding in the finale of the series *Sense8*, available on Netflix. In 2019, the Eiffel Tower played a major role in the spectacular music video for the latest hit of the French rap group PNL, which has been viewed by tens of millions of people. The list of French and international blockbusters that cite the Eiffel Tower in their end credits goes on and on…

Her success is partially due to the fact that she films well… Not to mention that her eternally modern and unique architecture inspires filmmakers just as it has always sparked the imagination of painters, poets, musicians, artists, and great fashion designers. But above all, the Eiffel Tower's status has changed over the years. It is no longer simply the "highlight" of the 1889 Universal Exhibition or the tallest structure ever built by man. It is no longer simply an unrivaled technological feat and the manifestation of France's incredible engineering and scientific minds at the dawn of the 20th century. The Eiffel Tower is much

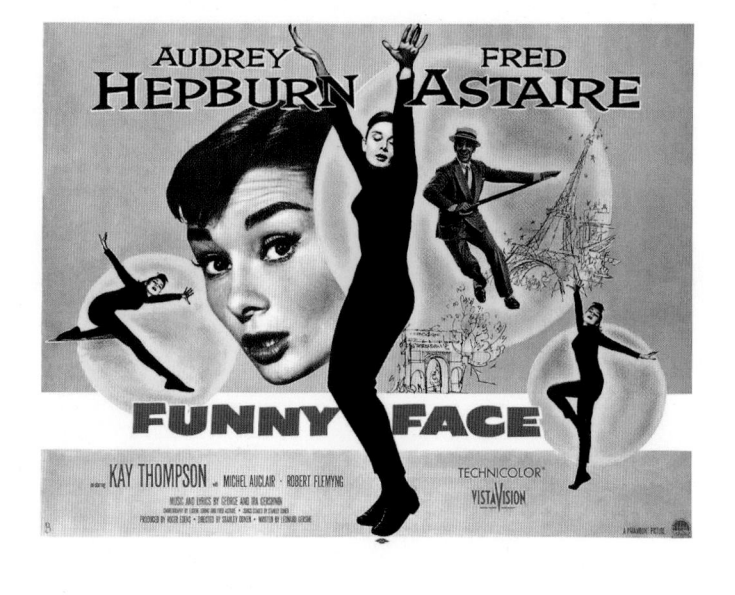

From the poster for the film *Funny Face* to the Las Vegas Strip, the Eiffel Tower makes an appearance everywhere – or almost everywhere.

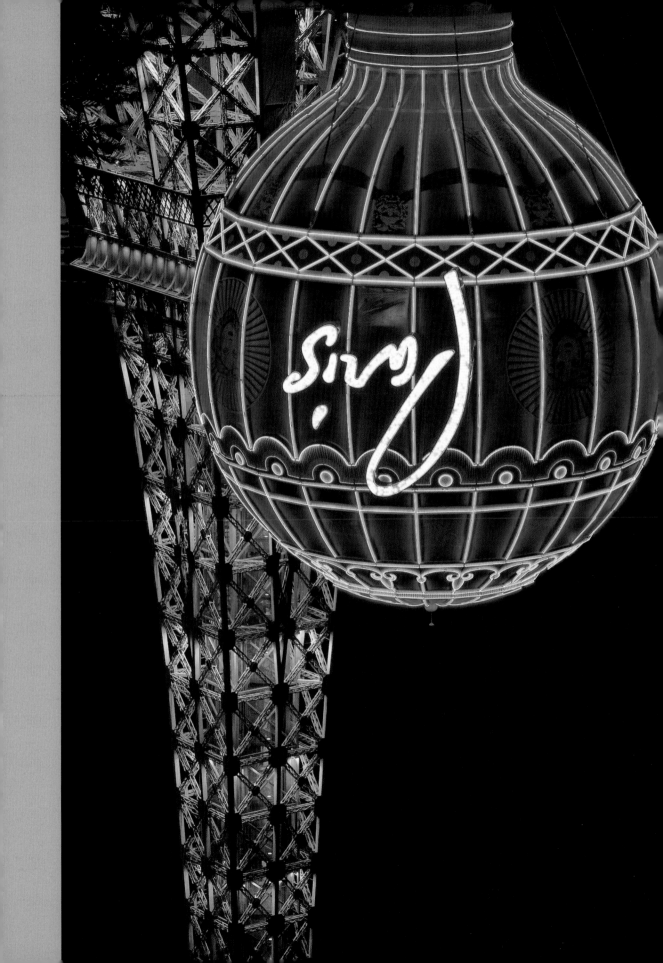

LIFE

MARCH 18, 1946 **10** CENTS
YEARLY SUBSCRIPTION $4.50

more than all of that: it has become a veritable symbol.

First and foremost, it has come to symbolize Paris, as suggested by its more or less discreet image on the logos of many major brands and official events, such as the Galeries Lafayette, the Paris airports, the Paris Saint-Germain soccer club, COP21, and the 2024 Olympic Games, in which the Tower will play an important role. The Tower has also come to represent the country itself, to the extent that its image is often used to symbolize France abroad. Last but not least, the Tower embodies values related to culture, elegance, modernity, and international solidarity. The SETE (*Société d'exploitation de la tour Eiffel*) strives to reinforce all of the many facets of this universal icon, by modifying the Tower's lighting for international celebrations and tragedies, for example, or by organizing a design competition in 2019 for objects (everyday or otherwise) related to the monument as a way to showcase the talent of young designers, artisans, and couturiers and to encourage the unique blending of emotion, innovation, expertise, and imagination that continues to make the Tower eternally modern.

An airline wants to promote its routes to Paris. So what does it feature on the poster? The Tower, of course.

TOP RIGHT

Jean Carlu, *To Paris via Pan American, The World's Most Experienced Airline*, 1954.

Blue, white, red ...The Eiffel Tower is Paris, and Paris is France. Model Vanessa Demouy
displays a miniature Eiffel Tower at the Balmain fashion show, marking
the bicentenary year of the French revolution, 1989.

The Eiffel Tower is still there
Hello Tower, hello, hello Paris
There are pigeons on the Opera Garnier
Notre-Dame still has two towers
The Seine is still in its bed
And Pont Neuf hasn't aged a day
On the benches of the Luxembourg
People still proclaim their love
There's still hope, ladies
The Eiffel Tower is still there!

Literal translation of an excerpt
from Mistinguett's song,
"La tour Eiffel est toujours là," 1942

It looked very different from the Statue
of Liberty, but what did that matter?
What was the good of having
the statue without the liberty?

Josephine Baker upon seeing the Eiffel Tower

AN ENDLESS SOURCE OF INSPIRATION FOR CREATIVE MINDS

Although the Tower and artists didn't exactly get off on the right foot – let's not forget their initial cries of fury and outrage – their relationship soon turned into a long and intense love story. Thanks to these creative poets, writers, painters, musicians, filmmakers, photographers, couturiers, and the list goes on, this "iron muse of a new world" would become an allegory for modernity and the avant-garde before incarnating Parisian elegance itself. Apollinaire would turn her into a shepherdess watching over her "flock of bridges." Aragon would describe her as a "lady with an envy-inducing corset." The Cubist Robert Delaunay was undoubtedly one of her greatest admirers among painters, although Seurat, Bonnard, Utrillo, Signac, Chagall, Rivière, Dufy, and Léger (to cite a few) also contributed to making the Tower into an international icon. This status would prompt fashion designers to envelop the monument in a new esthetic layer. Chanel, Kenzo, Hermès, Dior, Vuitton, Givenchy, and Jean-Paul Gaultier: the greatest in the fashion industry have associated themselves with the Tower.

OPPOSITE
The Tower serves as backdrop to René Clair's film *Paris qui Dort* (1924).

ABOVE
Cover for *Vogue* magazine from the 1920s.

THE TOWER AND THE SILVER SCREEN

Born at the same time as cinema, the Tower, like any self-respecting international star, has worked with the industry's greatest filmmakers. As early as 1897, the Lumière brothers executed the world's first vertical tracking shot at the Tower. The Iron Lady would go on to inspire many others, from René Clair to Ernst Lubitsch, from Louis Malle to James Ivory, and from François Truffaut to Chris Marker.

AN ANIMATION STAR

When Disney comes to Paris, it is nearly impossible to pass up the actress who embodies the City of Lights. In *The Aristocats*, *Cars 2*, and above all, *Ratatouille*, the Tower can be seen overlooking the capital's rooftops. The Tower is also featured in other animated films such as *Anastasia*, *The Triplets of Belleville*, *Dilili à Paris*, etc.

Roger Moore as Agent 007 in *A View to A Kill*.

Jean Marais with a pair of dancers on the Trocadéro esplanade.

For its haute couture catwalk show in 2017, Chanel replicated the Tower in the heart
of another celebrated Paris monument, the Grand Palais.

THE EIFFEL TOWERS OF THE WORLD

Such is the fate of all icons whose influence and popularity stir up a mixture of admiration and lust that prompts some to try to claim them. For the last 130 years, reproductions (with varying degrees of success) and imitations (which often pale by comparison) have sprouted up all over the world. In fact, it didn't take long. As early as 1890, British authorities organized a competition to build a metal tower in London… measuring 1,181 feet in height. Numerous proposals were immediately submitted – all of which were very similar to the original model, to the extent that the jury eventually concluded that "the Eiffel Tower unites the most rational and obvious means to building a monument that is both architectural in appearance and economical in construction." The English project would never actually come to fruition. This misadventure did not, however, discourage the rest of the world. From the United States to China and from Russia to Brazil, the replicas (of varying size) of this Parisian monument are countless. That being said, the reproduction in Las Vegas is undoubtedly the most successful and the tallest. Incidentally, Eiffel Towers have also been built in Texas, Tennessee, and even Russia in cities that also bear the name… Paris.

Often copied but never equaled. There are replicas of the Tower all over the world: seen here in Tokyo in Japan (top right), in Las Vegas in the United States (below right) and in Macao in China (opposite page).

THE TOWER AS A WORLD CITIZEN

He's all alone in the middle of the open sky on a wire measuring barely an inch in diameter 328 feet above the ground… On August 26, 1989, as the astounded crowd and television viewers from all over the world watch in stupefaction, the tightrope walker Philippe Petit crosses the 2,297 feet that separate the first floor of the Eiffel Tower from the Trocadero. In his hands, a copy of the 1789 *Declaration of the Rights of Man*.

That year, as France celebrates its two hundredth anniversary of the French Revolution, the Tower (which has just turned one hundred) obviously plays a central role in the festivities, as it does for joyful and tragic events in France and abroad. The Iron Lady, this familiar and universal symbol, has a dress for every occasion: fiery red for the Chinese New Year, Japanese motifs to celebrate a year of cultural exchange between France and Japan, the French flag's blue, white, and red to join in the celebration after a World Cup soccer victory. Her comforting beauty and soundness also accompany the people of the world during times of mourning or fear. By wearing the colors of countries struck by terrorism or catastrophe or by turning out her lights completely, the Iron Lady is a symbol of France's solidarity and support.

WHEN THE TOWER DANCES…

From Charles Trenet to Mistinguett, Artur H, Jacques Dutronc, Léo Ferré, and Pascal Obispo, the Tower's praises have been sung by the greatest. And some have had the privilege of giving a concert at its feet, always a grandiose event. Take, for example, Édith Piaf (from the first floor for the premiere of the film, *The Longest Day*), Georges Brassens, or Charles Aznavour. The most memorable shows, however, are still those performances given by Jean-Michel Jarre in 1995 for UNESCO's 50th anniversary; The Three Tenors (José Carreras, Placido Domingo, and Luciano Pavarotti) on July 10, 1998 before 200,000 people; David Guetta in 2016 during the Euro… and of course Johnny Hallyday, who figuratively set the Champ-de-Mars on fire on June 10, 2000 before an audience of more than 600,000 people.

OPPOSITE
Fireworks on 14 July 2015.

TOP LEFT
In 1989, on the Tower's 100th anniversary, the acrobat Philippe Petit tightrope-walked the 2,297 feet that separate the Tower from the Trocadéro.

SHOWS AND LIGHTS: GOING ALL OUT

It's a must in Paris's social calendar. Every 14th of July, the Eiffel Tower offers tourists and Parisians an unforgettable fireworks display. Then again, the monument, the French national holiday, and pyrotechnics are old friends. In 1888, before Eiffel had even definitively finished the Tower, the first rockets and flares were set off from the second floor of the work in progress. A little over 100 years later, in June 1989, the Tower celebrated its centennial with an incredible show featuring lasers, singers, dancers, and acrobats. But the most memorable of all was undoubtedly the extraordinary fireworks display to celebrate the year 2000. Broadcast live on more than 250 television channels throughout the world, this amazing show was not something that its spectators are likely to forget. Ever since, having mastered the art of using the Tower's slender structure, its silhouette, and its voids, pyrotechnics specialists compete to dream up the most creative, audacious, and spectacular shows yet, blending together video projections and explosions of light. Simply breathtaking.

1

METRIC TON. THE COMBINED WEIGHT OF ALL OF THE ROCKETS AND OTHER PYROTECHNICS USED FOR THE FIREWORK DISPLAY AT THE TOWER ON JULY 14, 2018

PULLING OUT ALL THE STOPS FOR 130 YEARS

To celebrate its 130th birthday, the Eiffel Tower went all out with an incredible light show retracing its history. In addition to the tens of thousands of spectators, this event was also extensively shared via social networks. And so, as it has always done, the Eiffel Tower looks to the future without ever forgetting its past. Perhaps that's the secret of its longevity and its place of honor, in the skyline of Paris and across the rest of the world…